Chef and the Fatman

RED, WHITE & BLUE (COLLAR) COOKIN'

Written By:
Kevin Jenkins
Fred Genovese

Published by:
Erik Holdo

ISBN 1-4276-1131-9

To my father and mother,
Robert and Rosemary Jenkins
who gave me the inspiration to appreciate
GREAT food and reach for the stars.

To she "Who Must Be Obeyed": my wife,
best friend, engineer, and, "biggest fan",
Karen Jenkins.

FOREWARD

By Kevin Jenkins

Wow…who would have thought it. Here I am writing a foreword for our first cookbook of what we hope will be many. I write like I speak -*lengthy*, so bear with me. I hope you enjoy this "insiders" look into the Chef and the Fat Man Red, White and Blue (Collar) Cookin' cookbook.

This cookbook came about as a spin-off of our radio show "Chef and the Fat Man the Blue Collar Chefs". The idea was born over five years ago at a radio station remote broadcast. A very forward thinking PD (program director), Mike Thompson, was at the radio station I was working for at the time. Mike is a very successful PD and an out-of-the-box thinker when it comes to radio (thank God).

We had been discussing food, as we were both rather portly at the time. It was true "common ground". He said there had been a very successful "food show" in Philadelphia that a rather seasoned couple had been doing for a number of years.

I liked the idea, but suggested a twist. I wanted to go back to the golden era of radio. Although I am too young to have heard programs such as "The Shadow", "The Green Hornet", "Gunsmoke" and "Suspense" first hand, I became hooked on recordings of them at a young age. These creative shows left an indelible image on my mind. Armed with Mike's suggestion, I spun this wild idea of taking the very best of old time radio, what I refer to as "Theatre of the Mind", into an actual "cooking" radio show. We would broadcast before live audiences (just like the old shows), and let the natural sound of chopping, stirring, food processing, pans crashing… well…you get the idea. We'd let the environment become our "Foley artists". The sound effects would enhance the listener's experience. It was a way to reintroduce our listeners to their imaginations while having fun, being very informative, and giving great recipes.

We started out by developing the recipes ourselves. We used our imagination, or tweaked great recipes we had researched or been given, mixing in our personalities as a fundamental ingredient. Then we added restaurant reviews (developing the best review team in the country, I might add) in which we cut more new ground by doing only POSITIVE reviews. We wanted to tell people WHERE to go, not where NOT to go. Very quickly, through our restaurant reviewing, we met a certified European wine and spirits expert who just happened to have not only the same playful attitude, but also the driving passion that we had. *Voila*! Andy Stangenberg became the third person in our on-air-team.

In order to do the shows live every week we needed a lot of equipment and a "take charge" person to make sure it all came together. That person also needed to be able to edit the show to perfection for airplay. "She Who Must Be Obeyed", my wife Karen, took the reigns as board operator, producer, editor, and, all around gadget gal for our show for the last three years. Without her, we would not be where we are today.

Recently we added another wonderful dimension to our team, Erik Holdo. Not only did he get us streaming on the web so more fans could reach us, Erik became our fill-in chef when Fred couldn't make it and fill-in Engineer when Karen couldn't make it. He is also the editor and publisher for this book, so blame him for the typos!

Now, I must say a few words about Executive Chef Fred Genovese -*he is the man!* When we started, he was the culinary brain working behind the scenes of our first, short-lived, person I had in the chef's spot. I did not know until we took to the air that it was Chef Fred who had the brains and talent for the recipes. We became fast friends.

He quickly took over as "The True Chef" (having graduated from a top culinary school in Atlanta). Over the years, Chef Fred has developed an on-air personality that mirrors his fabulous culinary skills. Most importantly, he has become the best friend and partner anyone could hope for. As you delve into these recipes, you will see that they at times seem very simplistic. You're right! They are! These recipes are meant to be "easy and tasty". It takes an artist to make the most difficult things seem easy. Chef Fred (the Goombah of Goodness) has simplified the complex to make everything more approachable to the average home chef. This is why I refer to him as, "The Man".

By the way, this is no diet cookbook! You will see in most of these recipes, we never use "weenie" ingredients. Only the best tasting ingredients, such as real butter, real cream…. ahhhhh! …only these will be used. No soy substitutes for meat! No yogurt substitutes for cream! Feel free to modify them, if you must, but remember, these recipes can only be certified "Fat Man good" if you use the real stuff!

Five years ago there were many who thought this concept wouldn't work . Well, we're still here and have grown from a 1500-watt (small station) to a 50,000-watt (large station) in Atlanta, Georgia. We are currently in discussions involving other stations for the Chef and the Fat Man Radio Network…stay tuned!

Now that you know our staff and our history, I hope you understand where we came from. We have evolved to a point in our career that a lot of people are asking for our recipes (even though they are on the web along with streaming audio of our shows, www.chefandhthefatman.com). The time has come to compile some of our best and favorite recipes, along with some recipes from our favorite chefs we have interviewed or worked with over the years.

The title the "Chef and the Fat Man Red, White and Blue (Collar) Cookin'" was arrived at pretty simply. We owe so much to our country for the freedom we are granted to make this cookbook, have a radio show and to have traveled so freely across this great country. We've met awesome people like Chef Rafih, owner of Atlanta's incredible Imperial Fez restaurant, who taught us love for food and your fellow man go hand-in-hand; to Lou Giglio (worldwide ambassador for Southern Comfort gone from this earth, but always in our hearts); Ann Rogers (owner of Sponsorship One, a top PR company in New Orleans); Chef Duke LoCicero (owner of Café Giovanni in New Orleans); Chef Tommy DiGiovanni (Executive Chef of Arnaud's, one of New Orleans greatest restaurants!); and, Marvin, the Magnificent (bartender extraordinaire) of the famous Carousel Bar in the gorgeous Monteleone Hotel (our official place of residence when in New Orleans), who showed us why New Orleans, like America is so awesome. It's the people, soul, heart, and, freedom we have to raise a city from ashes to magnificence like the proverbial Phoenix without whining or crying. Just hard work, drive, dedication and good old American Red White and Blue Values.

To our fabulous American Troops and first responders everywhere…we owe YOU so much and as we like to remind our listeners each and every week at the end of our show. "Please pray for our Troops and first responders as they are the reason we enjoy the freedoms we have…the price of freedom…. is NEVER FREE."

From our "loving family" at the Chef and the Fat Man, the Blue Collar Chefs to yours…. Mangia!
You can now hear Chef and the Fatman 24 and 7 on iRadioNow.com. Check us out!

To my soul mate and true love of my life, my wife Linda.

To my dad, whom I lost to cancer in '03. He taught me the art of trying new things and to never doubt the power within you. I miss you.

I love you both tremendously…Fred

FOREWARD
By Fred Genovese

It all started with one man's dream and passion for radio. We hooked up and I soon realized the "Fat Man", Kevin, was really serious about this thing he called "theatre of the mind", a true cooking show on radio. Well, it needed a name and I was a chef and he was fat! The Chef and the Fatman show was born.

Our first show was done in front of about 10 people. That had to be the fastest two hours of my life. I was hooked. As time progressed we worked out lots of kinks, and the show grew. With great support from our wives and family we continued on this journey, never knowing what lay ahead. We have had the great opportunity to work with both celebrity chefs from TV and local chefs in the trenches, both producing great food with that personal passion.

Well, I guess that after five years on the air, a cookbook is our next step. We wanted this cookbook to be fun and easy, much like us. After all, we try to de-mystify cooking because we are "the blue-collar chefs". This book is designed to help you get your family back to the dinner table. These recipes will hopefully serve as a base to create your own family treasures. Remember, cooking is meant to relax and get your creative juices flowing. It is ok to fail, just learn from your mistakes and don't have your family be the lab rats, taste as you go. Try new things.

If you wouldn't mind, please take a moment to say thanks for our troops and first responders that have given us the incredible freedoms we enjoy each day, for they pay the ultimate price for us. Remember, the price of freedom is NEVER FREE.

MANGIA !! MANGIA !!

A special tribute to the **ULTIMATE COOKING VESSEL**,
the **Big Green Egg (BGE).**

In our infancy as a show, Chef Fred began researching grills as we knew that grilling, smoking and outdoor cooking was going to be an integral part of our show.

Chef contacted a very kind and savvy businessman and entrepreneur, Ed Fisher, the owner of the Big Green Egg (BGE). Chef met with Ed and the two hit it off. We started our "Eggventure" shortly after their meeting and the rest has been history.

We have performed so many recipes on the BGE, which, if we tell you to preheat your oven or to fire up the grill or smoker, we really mean you should use the BGE. If you do, you will find what we have…. any type of cooking on the BGE is better than cooking indoors or on any other grill.

Throughout the years we wouldn't have been able to "Eggsperience" the success we have had with the Egg or our show without the unflappable help, assistance, and, the classy can-do attitude of our Big Green Egg "family": Jim Nufer, John Creel, Lou West, and, the "Lady in Egg Green", Brenda. These folks truly are and live the BGE dream day-in and day-out.

To Ed Fisher and our whole "Egg family", we say thank you for creating the BGE and, most of all, thank you for your loyal and unwavering support of our show.

Chef and the Fat Man Staff:
Executive Chef-Fred Genovese
Host/Show Creator- J. Kevin Jenkins
Wine and Spirits Expert-Andy Stangenberg
First Engineer/Producer-Karen "She Who Must Be Obeyed" Jenkins (my wife)
Second Engineer/Producer/Technical Advisor/Publisher/Chef-Erik Holdo
Executive Sous Chef-Mike Stock
Web Designer and Consultant-Deanne Stock

Chef and the Fatman
The Recipes !!

A

APPLE DUFF

4 Apples
2 ounces brown Sugar
2 ounces Raisins
Cinnamon to taste
1 Egg, beaten
1/2 pint Cream, whipped
1 package Puff Pastry (12 oz)

Preheat oven to 350 degrees.

Mix brown sugar, raisins and cinnamon together in a bowl.

Peel and core the apples.

Stuff the centers with the mixture of brown sugar, raisins and cinnamon.

Roll out the pastry and cut out 4 circles approximately 8" in diameter, depending on the size of the apples.

Place an apple in the center of the pastry circle and brush the edge with beaten egg; draw up the pastry to enfold the apple, pressing the edges firmly to seal.

Brush the tops of the pastry parcels with the remaining egg to glaze.

Bake in a shallow ovenproof dish for 40 minutes.

Serve with whipped cream.

Desserts

Notes:

APPLE SCRAMBLE

2 cups plus 3 1/2 tablespoons all purpose Flour
3 Eggs
1 1/2 cups plus 1 1/2 tablespoon Milk
1 teaspoon
Salt
Sugar to taste
3 Apples peeled, cored, and diced
7 tablespoons Butter
Powdered Sugar for dusting

Combine the flour, eggs, milk, a bit of sugar and salt. Stir into a smooth dough.

In a skillet, melt the butter and lightly sauté the apples.

Pour the dough over the apples.

Constantly stirring the whole with an egg turner, cook until the 'Kratzet' has browned all around.

Dust with sugar, and serve.

Desserts

Notes:

3

AWESOME HOT FUDGE TOPPING

Serve at approximately 140 degrees according to aficionados. Serve it the way you like it. The cooler the thicker.

3/4 cup Butter
1 cup Sugar
1/2 cup evaporated whole Milk
5 ounces Cocoa powder (10 Tablespoons)
4 ounces milk Chocolate (chips or solid)
1/8 teaspoon Salt
1 teaspoon Vanilla

Combine all ingredients except vanilla in a microwave proof bowl. Microwave on 50% power for 10 minutes, stirring occasionally, until bubbly and very thick. Remove from microwave and stir in vanilla. Store in glass container in refrigerator.
You can also do this on the stove top on medium high heat with a double boiler, stirring frequently, until smooth.

Desserts

Notes:

4

B

BACON WRAPPED PORK TENDERLOIN

1 medium Pork tenderloin
1/2 pound pepper seasoned thick cut Bacon
Chef and the Fatman Love Rub or any other favorite rub
Olive Oil

Preheat BGE to 300 degrees.

Clean silver skin from tenderloin.

Coat with olive oil and massage the meat with the rub.

Allow to rest at room temp for about 20 min.

Carefully wrap the bacon around the meat and place in preheated BGE.

Insert thermometer and set temp for 160 internal temperature.

When temperature is reached, remove the meat and let rest 10 minute.

Cover with a foil tent.

Meats

Notes:

BAKED RIGATONI

1 stick unsalted Butter plus 3 tablespoons diced
1/2 cup all purpose Flour
1 quart whole Milk
1 pinch fresh grated Nutmeg
White Pepper
1 cup grated fontina Cheese
1/2 pound thinly sliced Prosciutto(shredded)
1 pound dry Rigatoni

Preheat BGE or oven to 350 degrees.

To Make the Béchamel sauce:

In a 2 qt saucepan melt the butter over medium heat, then add the flour.

Whisk for about 2 minutes to remove flour taste and all lumps.

Slowly add the milk and increase the heat a little.

When the sauce can coat the back of a spoon, the sauce is almost ready. This

process will take about 10 min.

Grate in nutmeg and a handful of the Fontina cheese and the shredded Prosciutto.

Season with white pepper.

Set aside, placing a piece of heat-safe plastic wrap directly on the mixture, to
Prevent a "skin" from forming.

Cook the Rigatoni in salted boiling water until almost al dente. Drain.

In a large mixing bowl pour in the pasta and top with the béchamel sauce
(This is the time to add anything else to the dish- mushrooms, peas,
asparagus....).

Place pasta and cream sauce into a buttered baking dish.

Smooth out the top and add the cubes of butter and the rest of the cheese.

Bake in the oven for 25-30 minutes until golden brown.

Pasta

Notes:

BANANA NUT BREAD

1 3/4 cups all purpose Flour
2 teaspoons Baking Powder
3/4 teaspoon Salt
1/4 Baking Soda
1 cup mashed ripe brown spotted nanners (Bananas)
1/2 cup Milk
1 teaspoon Vanilla
1/2 cup solid Shortening
1 cup Sugar
2 large Eggs
1 cup Pecans (or nuts of choice)
raisins, seedless (optional)
cinnamon (optional)

Preheat BGE or oven to 350 degrees.
Whisk the flour, baking powder, baking soda and salt in a mixing bowl.
Using your Kitchen Aid mixer, begin creaming the shortening, and then add in the sugar. Mix well.
Add the eggs one at a time while mixer is running on slow speed.
Add in the bananas and vanilla, continue mixing.
Add the dry ingredients and mix until incorporated.
Transfer to buttered loaf pan.
Place in the pre-heated oven and bake about 70 minutes.
Cool and then turn out onto a wire rack.

Desserts

Notes:

BANDITO WINGS

12 Chicken wings
1/2 teaspoon Salt
1/8 teaspoon Pepper
8 tablespoons Butter
2 tablespoons vegetable Oil
1/2 cup Taco Sauce
1/4 cup Barbeque Sauce
1/4 cup french Dressing
1/8 teaspoon Hot Sauce
1/8 teaspoon Worcestershire sauce

Preheat BGE or oven to 300 degrees.

Cut off and discard tips of each wing at first joint; cut apart the two remaining parts at the joint, sprinkle with salt and pepper.

Heat 2 tablespoons butter and the oil in large skillet over medium heat.

Cook half the wings in the butter mixture until golden, 8 to 10 minutes on each side.

Remove from pan and reserve.

Prepare the other wings in the same manner.

Melt remaining 6 tablespoons butter in 1-quart saucepan; blend in remaining ingredients.

Arrange wings in shallow baking dish.

Brush sauce over wings to coat evenly.

Bake until hot, 5 to 8 minutes.

Pour remaining sauce in bowl; serve as dip for wings.

Appetizers, Poultry

Notes:

BARBEQUE SAUCE FOR SHRIMP SKEWERS

Recipes provided by Executive Chefs Christopher and Clinton from the Mondo Mocha Cafe at the Doubletree Atlanta Northwest - Windy Hill Marietta, GA

1 cup Ketchup
1/4 cup Worcestershire sauce
3 tablespoons Leeks, minced
3 tablespoons fresh Garlic, minced
1/2 cup Pineapple juice
3 tablespoons Lemon juice
1/4 cup seasoned rice wine Vinegar
1/4 cup chopped fresh Cilantro
1/4 cup Hot Sauce
1/3 cup brown Sugar

Start by sautéing your leeks and garlic.

After they start to turn translucent, add the rest of the ingredients and bring to a boil until sauce begins to thicken.
Then use all you want baby! Pour on shrimp before, after, or during grilling on BGE.

Seafood

Notes:

BARBEQUED SHRIMP SKEWERS

Recipes provided by Executive Chefs Christopher and Clinton from the Mondo Mocha Cafe at the Doubletree Atlanta Northwest -Windy Hill Marietta GA.

6 large Shrimp (Wild Georgia Shrimp if available), peeled and deveined
1 tablespoon Paprika
1 tablespoon Chili Powder
1 tablespoon brown Sugar
1 tablespoon Old Bay Seafood seasoning
1 teaspoon Thyme, dried
1 teaspoon Oregano, dried
1 teaspoon Lemon pepper
1 teaspoon Garlic powder
1 teaspoon Onion powder
1/3 cup vegetable Oil
Bamboo Skewers

Preheat BGE to 350 degrees.

Combine all dry ingredients with oil and mix well.

Add shrimp and toss to coat, refrigerate for 30 minutes.

Take bamboo skewer (soaked in water for at least 30 minutes) and skewer one raw pineapple chunk followed by a red onion and shrimp at top of skewer. Repeat, depending on length of skewer.
Place on heat for 3 minutes.
Brush with barbeque sauce (see other recipe) and allow cooking for another 2 minutes.
Place shrimp skewer on a mound of pineapple slaw and top with a purée of chives and olive oil.

Seafood

Notes:

BASIC CHICKEN STOCK

Recipes provided by Executive Chefs Christopher and Clinton from the Mondo Mocha
Cafe at the Doubletree Atlanta Northwest – Windy Hill Marietta, GA

1 whole Chicken cut into 8 pieces
7 cups Water
1 large Onion (Fat men always leave the skin on. Old Polish way –
adds flavor)
4 stalks Celery
4 Carrots (skin on)
1 Bouquet garni (Parsley stems, Thyme, 8 Peppercorns, and a Bay
Leaf) wrapped in cheesecloth

Wash the chicken to get rid of any blood and bone particles.
In a large stockpot add all ingredients.
Bring to a boil uncovered.
Skim any foam that comes to the surface.
Reduce heat to a low boil and simmer 2-3 hours, up to 8 hours, adding
water as necessary.
Strain stock thru a cheesecloth lined strainer or chinois.
Cool and remove fat.
Use in sauces and in place of water in other recipes.

Poultry, Soups, Stews and Chili

Notes:

BBQ NACHOS

1 large or 2 medium Pork tenderloin
1 bag Tortilla Chips
2-3 smoked Tomatoes, chopped
Fresh grated jack Cheese
Sour Cream
Black Olives, sliced
BBQ Sauce (to inject into the meat)

Preheat BGE or oven to 350 degrees.
Lightly smoke the tenderloin using pecan or maple wood on your Big Green Egg for 35 minutes.
Smoke 2-3 large whole tomatoes on BGE with tenderloin or in a smoker. Smoke for 10 minutes max.
Arrange chips on a plate or sizzle pan that can withstand the heat of a 350 degree grill.
When the pork is done remove from the BGE or oven and let it rest.
While the pork is resting, grate your cheese and chop your smoked tomatoes.
Slice the tenderloin thin and arrange on the chips.
Top with sour cream, olives, tomatoes and cheese.
Place plate onto the BGE or under broiler and let the cheese melt about 1-2 min.

Appetizers

Notes:

BISON MEATLOAF

Before starting this recipe please note a few things. Bison is extremely lean so therefore you will need to add a little fat (which is not a bad thing). Secondly, make a patty before you make a meatloaf to taste for seasoning. We topped our loaf with the rest of the ground sausage (just a thought)

2 1/2 pounds ground Bison
1/2 pound andouille Sausage
2 Eggs, beaten
1/2 cup Ketchup
1/2 cup Vidalia or yellow Onions, chopped
Salt and Pepper to taste
1/4 cup Breadcrumbs, plain

Preheat BGE or oven to 350 degrees.

Render the sausage to get rid of excess fat.

Remove sausage and carefully pulse in the food processor until it looks like ground beef.

Mix ingredients and chopped bison together in a large mixing bowl.

Place back into the refrigerator for at least 30 minutes (an hour is better).

Make a small patty and fry in a small fry pan. Taste cooked patty for salt, Seasoning, and moisture adjust to taste. If test patty tastes good, form meat mixture into a bread loaf form, then place into a 9x5 loaf pan and place into BGE. Add seasonings and/or ketchup if test patty was too bland or dry.
Cook until internal temperature of 150 is reached (about 1 hour).

Remove from pan and rest about 15 minutes under a foil tent.

Meats

Notes:

BLACK BEAN SAUCE TOFU

This recipe comes from friend Chef/Owner Kong of Atlanta's premier Chinese restaurant Little Szechwan.

1 package soft Tofu, cut in half the long way 3 times and then turn and cut 3 more times so they look like domino pieces.
2 tablespoons peanut Oil
1 teaspoon chinese black Beans
1 tablespoon Soy Sauce
1 teaspoon Oyster Sauce
1 Jalapeno, chopped
7 tablespoons Chicken Stock
1/2 teaspoon Garlic, chopped
1/2 teaspoon Ginger, chopped
1 pinch Sugar
1/2 teaspoon sesame Oil
2 teaspoons green Onions, chopped
1 tablespoon Corn Starch and Water (combine to make a slurry)
Asian sweet Rice (or other rice)
Roasted Sesame Seeds to taste
Green Onion pieces to taste

Heat wok or stir fry pan.
Add oil, Chinese black beans, garlic and chopped ginger stir. Fry until this becomes fragrant (3-4 minutes).
Add soy sauce, oyster sauce, jalapeño, chicken broth and tofu. Cook for 8 - 10 minutes.
At the end, add cornstarch and water slurry, sugar, sesame oil and chopped green onions and cook one more minute.
Serve with Asian Sweet Rice and sprinkle with roasted sesame seeds and fresh green onion sections.

Veggies

Notes:

BLACKENED FLANK STEAK DEGLAZED WITH WINE AND BLEU CHEESE

1 flank Steak (cut in half across the grain to fit your skillet)
1 tablespoon olive Oil
Salt and Pepper to taste
2 tablespoons Chef and the Fatman Love Rub
1 cup Shiraz Cabernet (plus a glass for the chef!)
2 tablespoons bleu Cheese

Season meat with either salt and pepper or Love Rub.
Add oil to skillet, get VERY HOT - sear the seasoned flank steak for three (3) minutes per side.
Turn off flame and add the wine and blue cheese.
Move the flank steak around the pan to pick up the flavors of the blue cheese and wine until evaporated (about 1 minute).
Let the steak rest for 10 minutes before slicing VERY THIN - ACROSS THE GRAIN.
Makes the Worlds Finest Fajitas, Steak Sandwiches, or served just the way they are as a main course.

Meats

Notes:

BLEU CHEESE TARTAR SAUCE

This recipe comes from the Chefs Clinton Del Marcelle and Christopher Effa from the Mondo Mocha Cafe at the Doubletree Atlanta Northwest - Windy Hill in Marietta, GA.

1 cup Mayonnaise
1 cup sour Cream
1 tablespoon Hot Sauce
1 tablespoon Sugar
3 tablespoons green Olive, chopped fine
2 tablespoons dill Pickle, chopped fine
1/4 cup Bleu Cheese
2 tablespoons white Vinegar
2 teaspoons Old Bay Seafood seasoning

Stir all ingredients thoroughly.
Chill for at least 2 hours prior to serving.

Sauces/ Dressings and Gravies

Notes:

BLOODY MARY LONDON BROIL

Remember to slice the meat thinly on the diagonal.

2 cups Tomato juice
1/4 cup Worcestershire sauce
3 tablespoons prepared Horseradish
2 teaspoons Marjoram, dried
1 teaspoon Basil, dried Fresh
Pepper to taste
2 1/2 pounds London Broil

Preheat BGE or oven to 450 degrees.

In a bowl mix first 6 ingredients, mix well.

Place meat into a Ziploc bag and add the marinade.

Let it stand in the refrigerator for 2 hours or at room temp for 30 minutes.

Turn over every 15 minutes.

Remove the steak and discard the marinade.

Cook 8 minutes per side.

Let the steak rest about 10 minutes under a foil tent.

Meats

Notes:

BLUE CHEESE SLAW

Remember if you are going on a picnic to keep cold food cold and hot food hot to avoid getting sick.

1 cup Maytag Bleu Cheese
1 cup Mayonnaise
1 cup sour Cream
1 bag Coleslaw mix
Salt and Pepper to taste

In a large mixing bowl, mix together the mayonnaise and sour cream.
Fold in the crumbled Bleu cheese.
Toss with the cole slaw mix and season with salt and pepper.
Place in refrigerator for at least 6 hours, 24 hours is best.

Salads

Notes:

BRAISED SEA SCALLOPS IN MARSALA SAUCE

1 pound sea Scallops
1/2 cup Breadcrumbs
1 tablespoon Garlic powder
1 tablespoon olive Oil
1/2 cup Marsala Wine
1/4 cup heavy Cream

Mix breadcrumbs with garlic powder in shallow dish.
Coat the scallops lightly with the breading.
Heat a large skillet to medium heat and add the oil.
Lightly brown the scallops for about 1 minute per side.
Remove the scallops from the pan and set aside.
Remove the pan from the heat and add the Marsala wine.
Return the pan to burner and turn up to high heat.
Reduce the Marsala by 3/4 and add the heavy cream.
Return the scallops to the pan and reduce the cream until it coats the back of a spoon (about two minutes).
Serve immediately.

Appetizers, Seafood

Notes:

BREAD PUDDING

1 loaf of stale Bread (egg bread works the best)
2 cups Sugar
3 Eggs
1/2 cup Raisins (optional)
Milk (How much? Till moist, size of loaf determines)
1 teaspoon Cinnamon
1 tablespoon Vanilla extract
FOR WHISKEY SAUCE:
1 cup Sugar
1 stick Butter
1/2 cup Whiskey, or whatever liquor you want to use
1 Egg, beaten

Preheat BGE or oven to 350 degrees.

Tear or cut the bread into chucks and place into a big bowl. Add all the other ingredients.

Mix well. (It is great at this time to use your hands to mix it).

Place into a baking pan about 13x9 and place into the oven for about 35 minutes.

Use a toothpick to check for doneness.

While this is cooking, let's make a sauce.

Traditionally it is a whiskey sauce but you can change the liquor if you like.

Mix ingredients and add to a cold saucepan.

Add egg.

Turn on the heat very low and stir constantly.

When bread pudding is done, top it with the sauce.

Serve with Vanilla Bean Ice Cream.

Desserts

Notes:

BROWNIE SHORTCAKE

1 pack Fudge Brownie mix prepare according to instructions
1 large pack Strawberries
16 oz heavy whipping Cream
1/2 cup Sugar
1/2 cup Water

In a medium saucepan over medium-low heat, combine 1/2 cup sugar and 1/2 cup water to make simple syrup.
DO NOT BOIL!!
Add 5-8 washed and halved strawberries.
In a mixing bowl, whip the heavy whipping cream until stiff peaks form (add a little sugar if desired, but you will have enough with everything else).
Now cool down your strawberry syrup.
Let's build this baby!!!
On the bottom of a bowl, place 1 brownie square, add a little cream, and pour a little strawberry juice on top, then fresh berries.
Continue to build to your hearts content.
Enjoy!!

Desserts

Notes:

BUFFALO CRAB STUFFED CHICKEN DRUMETTES WITH BLEU CHEESE TARTAR SAUCE

These recipes are from the Chefs Clinton Del Marcelle and Christopher Effa from the Mondo Mocha at the Doubletree Atlanta Northwest – Windy Hill Marietta, GA.

6 large Chicken drumettes
4 oz blue lump Crab
1/2 cup Panko breadcrumbs (Japanese style bread crumbs)
1 tablespoon Cayenne pepper sauce
1/2 Lemon, juiced
1 Egg yolk
1 teaspoon yellow Mustard
1 teaspoon Mayonnaise
1 teaspoon seasoned Salt
1 teaspoon lemon Pepper
1 teaspoon Garlic powder

Heat oil to 375. Preheat BGE or oven to 350 degrees.

Cut the skin off of the bottom of the drumettes and peel away using a sharp paring knife.
Gently draw your knife against the bone sliding the meat towards the top or fat part of the drumette.
This will create a pocket for which to stuff your crab mixture into.
For the stuffing simply mix all the other ingredients into a bowl.

Stuff this mix into the pocket and pull the meat over leaving a small amount of bone exposed.
Deep fry for about 3 minutes until golden brown.

Place them on a sheet pan and sprinkle them with lemon pepper.

Bake for about 12 minutes until cooked through.

Serve with Bleu Cheese Tartar Sauce (see recipe in Sauce section).

Appetizers, Meats

Notes:

C

CAJUN SHRIMP WITH CHEESE GRITS

1 pound Shrimp , (Wild Georgia Shrimp) peeled and deveined
Chef and the Fatman Spicy Love Rub
2 cups Grits, white (Instant are OK, just adjust cooking times accordingly)
12 oz habanero jack Cheese
½ stick Butter

In a saucepan bring water to a boil.

Cook the grits according to package directions.

While both are cooking grate the cheese using a frozen Kitchen Aid box grater.

Why frozen?

Glad you asked, the friction from grating the cheese causes heat and will make the cheese crumble but not grate.

When the grits are done add the cheese, stirring to incorporate.

Cover until the shrimp are done.

In a large sauté pan begin melting butter.

Season the shrimp and begin cooking them in the butter on medium heat.

Cook 3-4 minutes or until they just turn pink throughout.

Place a big heaping pile of grits in the middle of plate and top with the shrimp.

Serve with sourdough bread.

Appetizers, Seafood

Notes:

CAJUN STYLE CRAWFISH SCALLION RICE CAKES

1 pound Crawfish tail meat, cleaned
2 pounds cooked Rice
2 large Eggs
1 bunch Scallions, chopped
1/2 pound parmesan Cheese
Salt and black Pepper
Flour for dredging
Vegetable Oil

Mix the crawfish, rice, eggs, scallions, and cheese in a large mixing bowl.
Form into patties.
Lightly coat in seasoned flour.
Fry in pan until golden brown.

Appetizers, Seafood

Notes:

CALAMARI SALAD

Timing is everything when cooking calamari. If you over cook it.... rubber bands instead of delicious tasty rings.

1 1/2 pounds Squid tubes, cleaned
2 tablespoons Lemon juice
1 tablespoon red wine Vinegar
1/3 cup extra virgin olive Oil
Salt and Pepper to taste
1 small red Onion, thinly sliced
1/3 cup Olives (choose your favorite pitless olive)
2 cups grape Tomatoes
2 stalks Celery
1 cup flat leaf Parsley

Cut squid into rings.

Cook squid in boiling salted water (about 45-60 seconds).

Tip: float a wine bottle cork in the water - it will help tenderize the squid.

Place in a cold-water bath to stop the cooking process.

When the squid is cool, pat dry.

Mix all other ingredients together.

Place squid in with all ingredients, cover and place in refrigerator for 1 hour.

Salads, Seafood

Notes:

CHEDDAR CHEESE SOUP

4 tablespoons Butter
1 large Onion
1/3 cup red and green bell Pepper
4 cloves Garlic
1/2 cup Flour, all-purpose
2 cups Chicken Stock
1 1/2 pint whole Milk
1 1/2 pint Cream
12 oz sharp cheddar Cheese
Bacon crumbles for garnish

In a large heavy saucepan melt the butter over medium heat.
Add the onion and peppers and sauté until soft.
Add garlic and sauté for 1 minute.
Add flour and cook for about 1 minute, stirring constantly.
Combine chicken stock, milk and heavy cream in a stockpot.
Slowly whisk the onion and pepper mixture into the stockpot.
Bring soup to a low boil and reduce the heat and stir until the soup thickens.
Add the grated cheese 1/2 cup at a time stirring constantly.
DO NOT ALLOW SOUP TO BOIL.
Garnish with bacon and serve.

Soups, Stews and Chili

Notes:

CHEF AND THE FAT MAN
"I GOT YOU BABE" NACHO CHEESE

1 pound Velveeta
2 cups cheddar Cheese, shredded
3/4 pound ground Beef
3/4 pound hot Italian Sausage
1 small Vidalia Onion, minced
1 can Cream of Mushroom Soup
1 can hot Jalapeno relish
1 teaspoon Chipotle powder
1/4 cup green Pepper, finely chopped
1/4 cup red Pepper, finely chopped
4 cloves Garlic, minced
2 Scallions, minced

Remove the sausage from the casing and crumble into browning pan.

Brown and drain ground beef with sausage, onion, and bell peppers.

Melt cheese over low heat in a separate saucepan.

Add soup and relish to cheese, and then add meat mixture.

Serve over tortilla chips.

Sauce can be put in crock-pot for a party or be frozen for use later.

Appetizers

Notes:

CHEF AND THE FAT MAN "LOVE THAT BLEU CHEESE" SALAD DRESSING

1 cup Mayonnaise
1 tablespoon Dijon-style mustard
2 tablespoons Onion, minced
1 tablespoon Garlic, minced
1/4 cup flat leaf Parsley, chopped
1/2 cup sour Cream
1 tablespoon Lemon juice
1 tablespoon distilled white Vinegar
1/2 cup bleu Cheese, crumbled
"Chef and the Fat Man Love Rub"

In a small mixing bowl, combine mayonnaise, onion, garlic, parsley, sour cream, lemon juice, vinegar and blue cheese.
Season with Chef and the Fatman Love Rub.
Cover and refrigerate for at least one hour before serving.

Salads

Notes:

CHEF AND THE FAT MAN "MANLY" PORK AND BEANS

Chef Hint: To de-gas beans, use the quick soak method. Boil beans in water for 2 minutes, then remove from the heat and let beans stand for 2-4 hours with the cover on. Or soak overnight for 12 hours. Next drain and discard the rinse water, then rinse again, and then cover with fresh cold water.

3 cans navy Beans, drained (reserve the liquid or 1 pound dry white navy beans rehydrated).
8 slices cured Bacon, maple or hickory smoked
1 3/4 pounds ground Pork or Beef or 3/4 lb. of each Pork and Beef.
1 medium Vidalia Onion
1/2 cup Ketchup
1/3 cup pure maple Syrup
1/4 cup dark brown Sugar
1 1/2 tablespoons Dijon mustard (or spicy brown mustard to make it more American)
1/4 teaspoon Cayenne pepper
2 Garlic cloves, minced
1 teaspoon Chipotle pepper (optional)
1 tablespoon Vinegar (optional)
1 tablespoon Worcestershire sauce
1 teaspoon sweet Paprika

Preheat BGE or oven to 300 degrees.
Cook ALL slices of bacon ½ way through, reserving 4 slices for later. Drain all bacon on paper towels.
Keep uncut strips separate.
Rough chop 4 slices; cut them up into to sizes you enjoy.
Brown meat.
Place beans in Dutch oven or flameproof casserole.
Add all remaining ingredients, to bean pot and mix well to combine.
Place in oven or BGE uncovered. Bake 3 hours, stirring every 1/2-hour for the first two hours.
After final stirring: Lay 4 reserved bacon strips on top, if desired. Cover tightly and bake 1 hour.

Meats, Soups, Stews and Chili

Notes:

CHEF AND THE FAT MAN AMERICAN ONION DIP

1/2 tablespoon Butter
1 cup Onion, chopped
2 tablespoons Worcestershire sauce
8 ounces sour Cream
1/2 cup Mayonnaise
1/2 teaspoon Salt
1/2 teaspoon Pepper
8 ounces cream Cheese, room temperature

In medium skillet, heat butter over medium-high heat until melted; add onion.

Cook and stir 3 to 5 minutes or until onions are tender and lightly browned.

Remove from heat. Stir in Worcestershire sauce. Cool completely.

In bowl, combine onion mixture, sour cream, mayonnaise, salt and pepper; and cream cheese. Mix until blended.
Cover and refrigerate at least 1 hour to allow flavors to blend.

Appetizers

Notes:

CHEF AND THE FAT MAN
AMERICAN RED DRESSING

1/2 cup Tomato soup, condensed
1/8 teaspoon Pepper
1/4 teaspoon Liquid Smoke flavoring
6 drops Tabasco
1/3 cup white Vinegar
3/4 cup extra virgin olive Oil
1 clove Garlic, minced
1/2 small Onion
1/2 cup Sugar
1 tablespoon dry Mustard
1 tablespoon Salt
1 tablespoon Worcestershire sauce
1/2 teaspoon Paprika
1/4 cup bleu Cheese, crumbled

Put all ingredients into blender and chop for one minute.

Continue blending until well mixed.

Pour into Mason jar and keep refrigerated.

Salads, Sauces/ Dressings and Gravies

Notes:

CHEF AND THE FAT MAN AWESOME GARLIC BREAD

1 cup Butter, softened
1 cup parmesan Cheese, grated
1/2 cup Mayonnaise
5 Garlic cloves, minced or juiced
3 tablespoons flat leaf Parsley, chopped
1/2 teaspoon Oregano, dry
1 loaf french Bread, cut lengthwise

Preheat BGE or oven to 375 degrees.

Mix all ingredients, except the bread in a bowl.

Spread the mixture on the french bread.

Wrap bread in aluminum foil.

Bake for 20 minutes.

Unwrap and place under broiler to brown.

Appetizers

Notes:

CHEF AND THE FAT MAN BARBECUED SHRIMP

2 pounds Shrimp, (Wild Georgia Shrimp if available) uncooked
1 Jalapeno, seeded and chopped
2 cloves Garlic, minced
1 teaspoon Paprika
1/2 teaspoon Salt
1 tablespoon fresh Ginger, minced
1/2 cup Soy Sauce
1/2 cup Lemon juice
3 tablespoons flat leaf Parsley, finely chopped
2 tablespoons Cilantro, finely chopped
1/2 teaspoon Pepper
melted Butter

Preheat BGE to 400 degrees.
Shell and devein shrimp, leaving tails on.

Arrange shrimp in shallow 1 1/2-quart dish.

In a small bowl, mix garlic with salt.

Stir in remaining ingredients.

Pour marinade over shrimp and refrigerate for at least 30 minutes.

Thread shrimp on skewers and grill 3 minutes, basting with marinade.

Turn and grill several minutes more or until shrimp turn pink, basting several times.

Seafood

Notes:

CHEF AND THE FAT MAN BRUNSWICK STEW

This is the "Best" you'll ever make. It took Chef and 1 2 months to get it to where we liked it.

3 pounds pulled Pork or shredded Chicken, cooked
1 28-32 oz can Chicken Stock
1 tablespoon Garlic, chopped
2 teaspoons coarse black ground Pepper
1 teaspoon Salt
1 teaspoon crushed red Pepper
1 ounce Liquid Smoke (won't need if cooking on Big Green Egg)
2 ounce Worcestershire sauce
2 ounce Crystal Hot Sauce or
1 ounce Tabasco
1/4 cup yellow Mustard
1 can (15 oz) Tomato sauce
1 tablespoon Lemon juice
3 medium Onions, chopped
2 cans (28 oz) Tomatoes, chopped and not-drained
2 Bay Leaves
3 small Potatoes, peeled and diced
3 tablespoons white Vinegar
1/3 cup Pork or Bacon drippings
1/2 cup Barbecue Sauce 1 cup Ketchup
1/2 cup Chili Sauce
1 3/4 cups whole kernel Corn, frozen
1/2 teaspoon Oregano, dried

Preheat BGE or oven to 300 degrees.
Place all ingredients (except the corn and the potatoes) into a large Lodge cast iron stockpot.
Season with salt, pepper, and hot sauce.
Cook, open, over light smoke in BGE stirring occasionally (every 1/2 hour) for at least 2 hours, or until thickened.
Stir the corn and potatoes into the stew mixture.
Continue cooking 1 hour, or to desired consistency.
Remove bay leaves.

Serve.

Soups, Stews and Chili

CHEF AND THE FAT MAN CHERRY CHEESE CAKE (COOKED)

2 package (8 oz) cream Cheese, softened
1/2 cup Sugar
2 tablespoons Flour
2 tablespoons melted Butter
1/2 teaspoon Salt
3 Eggs, slightly beaten
5 1/2 cup sour Cream
1/4 cup Lemon juice
1 teaspoon Vanilla extract
4 squares semi-sweet Chocolate, melted slightly
1 1/2 cups Cherry pie Filling
1 cup Whipped Topping, thawed
1 tablespoon Cherry flavored Liqueur
1 Keebler Ready Crust Graham Cracker Pie Crust (6 Oz. or 9 In.)

Preheat oven to 325 degrees.

Beat together eggs, sugar, vanilla, and sour cream.

Gradually add cream cheese, beating well.

Beat in melted butter.

Pour cheese mixture into 9-inch prepared and baked graham cracker crust.

Bake cherry cheesecake pie for 35 minutes, or until set in center.

Will firm up as it cools.

Top with cherry pie filling.

Chill for a couple of hours.

Desserts

Notes:

CHEF AND THE FAT MAN COCONUT MACAROONS

This is an awesome cookie for coconut lovers. "She who must be obeyed", my wife Karen, absolutely goes nuts over these.

14 ounce sweetened condensed Milk
3/4 cup Flour, all-purpose
14 ounces Coconut shreds, sweet
1/4 teaspoon Salt
2 teaspoons Vanilla extract
1 teaspoon Almond extract

Preheat oven to 350 degrees.
Use a good baking pan with baking paper if you wish.
In a mixer (or a large bowl) mix flour, coconut and salt.
Add condensed milk, vanilla and almond extract and stir well.
Make into 1 1/2 inch balls, and place 2 inches apart on a well-greased pan.
Bake for 13-18 minutes (depending on your ovens accuracy),
or until Macaroons are golden on top and bottom.
Take off pan right away and place on cooling rack.

Desserts

Notes:

CHEF AND THE FAT MAN CRAB STUFFED MUSHROOMS

4 portobello Mushroom caps, stems removed
16 ounces Crab Meat, fresh or canned
2 ounces parmesan Cheese
3 cloves Garlic, finely minced
4 slices provolone Cheese
8 ounces cream Cheese (room temperature)
1 ounce vegetable Oil

Preheat BGE or oven to 325 degrees.

In a mixing bowl combine (cleaned and picked through) crabmeat, parmesan cheese, garlic and any rub or spice you might like to add.
Wipe bottom of each mushroom cap lightly with oil then stuff the caps with crab mixture (lightly sprinkling rub or spice).
Take cheese slices and spread cream cheese heavily over one side of slice then flip it over on top of crab mixture in mushroom cap and repeat for other caps.
Place on BGE for approximately 15-20 minutes until cheese turns lightly golden brown.
Remove from Egg, and let rest for approximately 5 minutes.

Seafood

Notes:

CHEF AND THE FAT MAN EASY BUT DELICIOUS CHILI

2 pounds ground Beef (or ground leftover turkey)
1 Onion, sliced
16 ounces Tomato juice
4 ounces Tomato paste
16 ounces Tomato sauce
1 teaspoon Cumin
1 teaspoon Sugar
32 ounces kidney Beans
1 package McCormick Chili Hot Seasoning

Brown meat.

Sauté onions.

Combine above with the rest of ingredients (except Kidney Beans).

Bring to a boil then simmer for 3 hours.

Add beans during the last hour of cooking.

Soups, Stews and Chili

Notes:

CHEF AND THE FAT MAN GREAT GIBLET GRAVY

Giblets from Turkey (liver, heart, gizzard, and neck), cooked
4 cups Turkey Stock or broth, or chicken stock or broth
1 large Onion, chopped
2 stalks Celery, chopped
3 tablespoons flat leaf Parsley, chopped
2 Chicken Bouillon cubes
3 tablespoons Flour, all-purpose
3 tablespoons Butter
1/3 cup cold Water
Salt and freshly ground Pepper
1 Egg, hard boiled and sliced

While turkey cooks (or the day before), cook the giblets, wing tips, onion, celery parsley and neck bones with water in a large pot and simmer 2 hours.
Strain broth and reserve for gravy.
Pick meat from neck and wing tips; finely chop all giblets and meat.
Pour turkey drippings into bowl; let stand a few minutes or chill in refrigerator until fat rises to the top. Skim off the fat.
For each 2 cups gravy desired, use 3 tablespoons fat, measure fat into saucepan (Fat can be poultry fat, or butter), 3 tablespoons flour and 2 cups of liquid (meat juices or broth, vegetable juice, bouillon and/or water).
Over low heat, blend in flour; cook until bubbly, stirring constantly with a wire whisk. If desired, brown fat and flour slightly to give more color and flavor.
Remove pan from heat.
Stir in liquid and whisk constantly until blended with fat-flour mixture.
Add egg slices.
Add chopped giblets.
Simmer gently about 5 minutes.
Correct the salt and pepper to taste.

Sauces/ Dressings and Gravies

Notes:

CHEF AND THE FAT MAN HEAVY GREEN BEAN CASSEROLE

This is very easy and doesn't take as long as it seems.

4 cups green Beans, cut
2 tablespoons Butter
1 medium Onion, coarsely chopped
1 cup Mushrooms, sliced
1 can condensed Milk or Cream of Mushroom Soup (10 3/4-oz.)
1/2 cup Milk
1 can (2.8 oz) french fried Onions, divided
1 tablespoon Worcestershire sauce
1 teaspoon balsamic Vinegar
1 cup cheddar Cheese, shredded
1 cup parmesan Cheese plus ½ cup
1 teaspoon brown Sugar
1 1/2 teaspoons Dijon mustard
Salt and freshly ground Pepper to taste

Preheat BGE or oven to 350 degrees.
If using frozen green beans: blanch them in fast boiling water for 6 minutes then drain and pat dry before using.
If using fresh green beans snap, cut into bite size pieces and blanch for 4 minutes then drain and pat dry before using.
In a large frying pan melt the butter.

Add the onions and cook over medium heat, stirring occasionally, until they are translucent. If you have the time, go ahead and slightly caramelize the onions. While the onions are sautéing, add the mushrooms to the translucent onions and cook, stirring occasionally, until they give up their liquid and most of it has cooked off (they will get really slick looking and their size will reduce by 1/2).
Stir the soup, shredded cheddar cheese and the milk into the onion mixture.
Add about half the can of fried onions, stir in the Worcestershire, vinegar, brown sugar, mustard, salt and pepper. Stir in the green beans. Turn the mixture into a 1 1/2-quart casserole dish and bake 25 minutes.
Sprinkle the remaining half-can of onions and remaining Parmesan cheese over the top of the mixture and bake an additional 5 minutes, or put under broiler until top is browned.

Veggies

CHEF AND THE FAT MAN MUSTARD BBQ SAUCE

1/2 teaspoon Garlic powder
1/2 teaspoon Onion powder
1 cup yellow Mustard
1/2 cup balsamic Vinegar
1/3 cup brown Sugar
2 tablespoons Butter
1 tablespoon Worcestershire sauce
1 tablespoon Lemon juice
1 teaspoon Cayenne pepper (more if you want a better kick)

Mix all ingredients together and simmer over a low heat for 30 minutes.

This should make enough to fill a normal cheap plastic squeeze bottle plus a 1/3 rd.

Sauces/ Dressings and Gravies

Notes:

CHEF AND THE FAT MAN RED BBQ SAUCE

1 stick Butter
1 large Onion, chopped
6 cloves Garlic, minced
1 cup white distilled Vinegar (you may use apple cider vinegar for zingier taste)
1 teaspoon Cinnamon
2 cloves Garlic
1 tablespoon dry Mustard
1 teaspoon Chili Powder
1/2 cup brown Sugar (dark is fine)
2/3 cup Ketchup
1/2 cup Water
Salt and Pepper

Melt butter in a saucepan.
Add the chopped onion and minced garlic. Sauté until they just begin to brown.
Add white vinegar, cinnamon, whole cloves, dry mustard, chili powder, brown sugar and ketchup.
Stir, and then add water and blend.
Bring to a boil, lower heat to simmer add salt and pepper to taste.
Simmer for 20 to 30 minutes.
Strain or puree in food processor until proper consistency.

Sauces/ Dressings and Gravies

Notes:

CHEF AND THE FAT MAN SAUSAGE STUFFED BREAD

2 long Italian Hoagie Rolls, split and the dough removed
1 pound Sausage (breakfast or Italian)
1 small Onion, diced
1 small green Pepper, finely diced
1 Jalapeno, diced and seeds removed
8 ounces sour Cream
8 ounces cream Cheese (room temperature)
8 ounces cheddar Cheese, shredded

Preheat BGE or oven to 350 degrees.

In a large skillet begin browning the sausage until almost cooked.
Add the peppers and onion. Cook for 3 minutes.
Add the cream cheese, sour cream and shredded cheese. Mix well.
Fill the hollowed bread with the sausage stuffing.
Wrap loosely with foil and bake for 25-30 minutes.
Cut into pieces and serve.

Meats

Notes:

CHEF AND THE FAT MAN TOMATILLO SALSA

3 medium Tomatoes
7 Tomatillos
4 cloves Garlic
1 medium Onion, quartered
1 Chile, dried
1 bunch Cilantro
1/2 cup Lime juice
Salt to taste
Hot Sauce to taste

Griddle, roast or broil vegetables.
To griddle roast: place the tomatoes, tomatillos, garlic cloves, onion and chilies on a griddle or other heavy pan over medium heat.
After several minutes, the vegetables will begin to char.
Using kitchen tongs, rotate the vegetables so as to char them lightly all over.
Small chilies may broil much faster than tomatoes, so remove them when they're ready.
When the vegetables are cool enough to handle, peel the onion, garlic, tomatoes and tomatillos, discarding the charred husks.
Place the peeled garlic cloves, chilies, cilantro, salt, Chipotle and lime juice in the blender.
Pulse the blender repeatedly, until the garlic is a paste and the chilies and cilantro leaves are finely chopped.
Scrape down the sides of the blender if necessary.
If the mixture is too dry to process well, add a couple of tomatillos, or a tomato; either should contribute enough liquid to fix the problem.
Add the remaining tomatillos and pulse to break them up.
Then add the tomatoes and pulse just enough to break them up.
Pour the salsa into a non-reactive (glass, ceramic, or plastic) bowl.
Chop the onion into 1/4-inch diced pieces and stir them into the salsa by hand.

Taste for seasoning.
Stir in salt and/or hot sauce as desired.

Let the salsa stand for one hour at room temperature as the flavors combine.
Leftovers will keep for a few days, covered tightly, in the refrigerator.

Sauces/ Dressings and Gravies

CHEF AND THE FATMAN RANCH STYLE DRESSING

Recipes performed at the American Institute of Wine and Food (Atlanta Chapter) Annual Picnic and it was a real hit.

1 cup Mayonnaise
1/2 cup sour Cream
1 teaspoon Dill weed
1 clove Garlic peeled
2 tablespoons fresh Lime juice
1/4 cup Buttermilk
1 tablespoon fresh Parsley or Cilantro minced
1 tablespoon Chives snipped (or Onion Powder)
Hot Sauce to taste
Salt and Pepper to taste

Whisk (or shake) the ingredients until well blended.

Taste and adjust seasonings.

Cover and chill.

Makes approximately 1 1/2 cups.

Salads

Notes:

CHEF FRED'S 5 PUCKER POWER KEY LIME PIE

1 can (8 oz) sweetened condensed Milk
1 8 in graham cracker Pie Shell
5 ounces Nellie & Joe's Key Lime juice
3 Egg yolks

Preheat oven to 350.

In a mixing bowl combine egg yolks, Key lime juice and milk.

Stir to mix thoroughly.

Pour into pie shell and bake 15 minutes.

Remove and allow too cool.

When cool, cover and place in the refrigerator at least 4 hours (overnight is better but you may not be able to wait).

Slice and enjoy!

Desserts

Notes:

CHEF FRED'S DANCING HERB ROASTED CHICKEN

1 Chicken, whole fryer (2.5-3lb)
1/2 teaspoon each of Thyme, Oregano, Pepper, Salt, Cilantro and Cumin
1/2 cup extra virgin olive Oil

Preheat BGE or oven 350 degrees.

Mix your herbs.

Use the herbs you like. Just make sure they are all dry.

Rub chicken with olive oil and then rub with the herbs both inside and out.
Place on the tower of the BGE or on a roasting pan and cook until the internal temp at the thigh hits 180.
Let it rest.

Poultry

Notes:

CHEF MIKE'S APPLE CRISP

This recipe provided and performed by CFM Executive Sous Chef Mike Stock at Panorama Orchards in North Georgia.

3 pounds Apples, granny smith
2 tablespoons Lemon juice
1/2 cup brown Sugar
1/2 teaspoon Cinnamon
1/2 teaspoon Nutmeg
1/3 cup Flour, all-purpose
1/3 cup Sugar
1/3 cup rolled Oats
4 tablespoons Butter (cold)
1/2 cup Walnuts or Pecans, chopped

Preheat BGE or oven to 375 degrees.

Peel, core and chop apples, toss in a bowl with lemon juice to prevent darkening.

In a separate bowl, combine brown sugar, cinnamon, and nutmeg.

Stir into apples. Set aside.

In another bowl combine flour, sugar and oats.

Cut butter into 8 pieces, and cut butter into flour until mixture looks like crumbs.

Stir in nuts.

Butter a 10 X 10-inch baking dish.

Spread apples in bottom of baking dish. Sprinkle with flour mixture.

Bake for 45 minutes, or until apples are tender and topping is lightly browned.

Serve warm or at room temperature.

Desserts

Notes:

CHEF MIKE'S CHINESE GREEN BEANS

This recipe provided and performed at Frog Town Winery in Dahlonega, Ga by Chef and the Fat Man Executive Sous Chef Mike Stock.

1 pound absolutely fresh green Beans
3 quarts boiling Water
2 tablespoons dark sesame Oil
2 teaspoons sea Salt (fine grind)
1 pinch red Pepper flakes
2 teaspoons toasted Sesame Seeds

Tip and Tail the Absolutely snappy fresh green beans but leave whole.
Immerse in boiling water, wait until water re-boils and set timer for 3 or 4 minutes depending on the slenderness of the green beans.
Remove and drain beans at allotted time.
Shock the beans immediately in iced water to cool completely.
Dry the beans by shaking them in a clean towel.
Heat Sesame oil until 375 degrees in large Sauté pan or Wok and drop beans into pan.
Stir Fry until beans are slightly scorched, adding the salt and the pinch of red pepper flakes as you stir-fry.
Add the optional toasted sesame seeds right before serving.
DO NOT overcook beans in this last process.
Serve beans hot, warm or cold.

Veggies

Notes:

CHICKEN AND SHRIMP JAMBALAYA SALAD

These recipes were provided and performed by Chefs Clinton Del Marcelle and Christopher Effa from the Mondo Mocha Café at the Doubletree Hotel Atlanta Northwest - Windy Hill Marietta, GA

1 pound Chicken, cooked in blackened seasonings
1 pound blackened Georgia white Shrimp
3 cups white and brown Rice, cooked with blackened seasoning in water
1/4 cup Celery, diced
1/4 cup Onion, diced
1/4 cup bell Peppers, diced
1/4 cup Okra, pickled
1/4 cup cherry Tomatoes
3 tablespoons Garlic, minced
3 tablespoons Shallots, minced
1/2 cup andouille Sausage, cooked
1 1/2 cup Chicken Stock
1/2 cup white distilled Vinegar
1/4 cup Tomato paste

The sauce: start by sautéing the sausage over medium heat. After it starts to brown, add 2 tablespoons fresh butter, and then add 1/4 cup flour. Stir and allow cooking for a moment.
Add your chicken stock and vinegar.
Bring to a boil and add tomato paste.
Adjust salt and pepper as well as sweetness.
After 5 minutes, add celery, peppers and onions.
Cut off heat promptly.
Toss or arrange on a platter with all remaining ingredients.
Drizzle sauce and vegetables over the top.

Salads, Seafood

Notes:

CHIPOTLE SLAW

2 bags Slaw mix
1/2 cup Mayonnaise
2 teaspoons Lemon juice
4 tablespoons maple Syrup
Chipotle pepper to taste

In a medium-mixing bowl, combine all the ingredients except the slaw.
Taste and adjust the seasoning.
After you have the mixture the way you like, combine with the slaw mix.
Refrigerate and serve.

Salads

Notes:

CHOCOLATE BREAD PUDDING

2 1/2 cups stale Bread, large diced
1 teaspoon Vanilla
2 Eggs
2 tablespoons Cocoa powder
2 cups Milk
1 teaspoon Cinnamon
1/4 cup Sugar
3/4 cup Chocolate chips
Dash of Salt

Preheat BGE or oven to 350 degrees.

Place bread in a round, buttered, deep-dish pie plate.

In a medium bowl whisk together eggs, milk, sugar, a dash of salt, vanilla, cocoa and cinnamon.

Add chocolate chips.

Pour over bread and gently mix. Let sit for 15 minutes, so bread can absorb mixture.

Bake for 30 to 40 minutes until firm but not dry.

Desserts

Notes:

CHOCOLATE CHIP PECAN PIE

1 pre-made 9 inch Pie Shell
4 ounces Semi sweet Chocolate

2 tablespoons Butter
3 Eggs
1/3 cup Sugar
1 cup Corn Syrup, light or dark
1 teaspoon Vanilla Extract
1 1/4 cup Pecans, whole

Preheat BGE or oven to 350 degrees.

Melt chocolate and butter together in a double boiler.

Let cool slightly.

Beat eggs and add the corn syrup, chocolate mixture, sugar and vanilla.
Stir well.

Place into piecrust and bake for about 50-55 minutes, until a knife inserted comes out clean.

Cool pie before serving.

Desserts

Notes:

CHOCOLATE CHIP SCONES

3 1/4 cup Flour, all-purpose
1/2 cup Sugar
1 cup Baking Powder
1/4 cup Salt
1 cup Chocolate chips
2 cups whipping Cream
2 tablespoons Butter

Preheat oven to 375 degrees.
Combine the flour, sugar, baking powder and salt in a large bowl (sift if you wish).
Add the chips.
Beat cream using a Kitchen Aid stand mixer until firm peaks form.
Fold the whipped cream into the flour mixture.
Turn dough out onto lightly floured board.
Knead for about 2 minutes.
Pat out dough into 1-1/4 inch thickness.
Cut and place on buttered baking sheet.
Bake 15 minutes, brush with melted butter, and continue for another 5 minutes.
Serve warm.

Desserts

Notes:

CITRUS SHRIMP

1 pound Shrimp, peeled and deveined
Juice from 1 Lemon, Lime and Orange
Zest from Lime
1/2 bunch Cilantro

Preheat BGE to 350 degrees.
Place all items in a Ziploc bag and marinate for 1 hour. Shrimp will become tough if left in the marinade longer.
Place the shrimp on a skewer and place on the grill or Big Green Egg for about 4 minutes.
DON'T over cook.

Seafood

Notes:

CRAB AND CORN DIP

8 ounces cream Cheese, room temperature
8 ounces Crabmeat
1/2 teaspoon Horseradish, prepared
1/2 cup shredded parmesan or cheddar Cheese
Salt and Pepper to taste
1 ear Corn, fresh (take kernels off the cob)

Preheat the BGE or oven to 350 degrees.

Blend all ingredients together and place in a shallow baking dish.
Sprinkle with a little cheese and bake until bubbly and slightly brown,
approximately 25-30 minutes.
Serve with crackers or a strong chip.

Appetizers

Notes:

CRAB STUFFED PRAWNS

10 Prawns, peeled and deveined
8 ounces Crab meat
3 ounces Bread crumbs
1 large Egg
3 ounces parmesan/romano Cheese

Preheat BGE or oven to 350 degrees.
Place prawns in baking dish and season with Salt and Pepper.
In a mixing bowl mix the crab, breadcrumbs, egg and cheese.
Place mixture on top of prawns and bake for 18-20 minutes.
Serve 2 prawns for an appetizer or 6 for dinner.

Seafood

Notes:

CRANBERRY ORANGE COMPOTE

1/2 bag (6 oz) Cranberries, fresh
1/2 cup Sugar
Zest of 1/2 Orange
Juice from 1 Orange (1/2 used in first part of recipe)
1 pinch Cinnamon
1 cup Water
1/2 teaspoon Cornstarch

Zest orange before cutting in half or juicing, you will only need the zest from 1/2 of the Orange.
In a saucepan add first six ingredients.
Cook on high until the cranberries begin to pop open (do not overcook; cranberries get bitter if cooked too long).
Place the cornstarch in a small bowl and add the juice of 1/2 orange, whisking, to combine.
Add the cornstarch mixture to the saucepan and stir over medium heat.
Once it is thickened, remove from heat and let it cool slightly.
Place in a glass-serving bowl in the refrigerator till compote sets up.

Sauces/ Dressings and Gravies

Notes:

CRAWFISH AND RICE DRESSING

4 cups cooked Rice
1 1/2 pound Crawfish tail meat
1 pound andouille Sausage (optional)
Salt and Pepper to taste
1 cup green Onion, chopped

Preheat oven or BGE to 350 degrees.

This dressing is intended to be used to stuff a medium Turkey.

Wash your hands very well.

In a large mixing bowl combine all ingredients and mix by hand.

Pack inside of your bird or place in a casserole dish and bake for about 35-45 minutes covered (or until internal temperature of bird is at least 160 degrees).

Seafood

Notes:

CHORIZO ENCRUSTED
SEA SCALLOPS

8 ounces Chorizo Sausage, finely chopped
1/2 cup Breadcrumbs
16 large sea Scallops
1/2 cup Flour, all-purpose
2 Eggs, lightly beaten
3 teaspoons of olive Oil

In a hot sauté pan render the Chorizo for 2-3 minutes.
Remove from the heat and put in the food processor and pulse with the breadcrumbs until it binds.
Season the scallops and dredge in the flour, then dip into the beaten eggs, then dust in Chorizo and breadcrumbs.
Heat another skillet with olive oil until medium high heat. Pan-fry the scallops until golden brown.
Drain on paper towel and serve.

Appetizers

Notes:

CRAZY CAKE

This recipe is from my mother-in-law, Ms. Ada Sanders. A classic "dump some" cook. Nothing phoofy...just delicious.

1 1/2 cup Flour, all-purpose
1 cup Sugar
3 tablespoons Cocoa
1 teaspoon Baking Soda
1 teaspoon Salt
1 tablespoon Vinegar
6 tablespoons cooking Oil
1 teaspoon Vanilla
1 cup Water

Preheat oven to 350 degrees.

Sift dry ingredients once, then sift them again into an 8 or 9-inch square cake pan.

Make 3 wells in the flour.

In the first, put the vinegar.

In the second, put the oil.

In the third, put the vanilla.

Pour water over all the ingredients.

Stir with a fork until it is mixed well.

Bake for 25-30 minutes.

Ice with your favorite chocolate frosting.

Desserts

Notes:

CUCUMBER SOUP

4 large Cucumber, peeled, seeded and cut into medium pieces
2 cups Yogurt, plain
4 leaves fresh Mint
2 teaspoons Honey

In a Kitchen Aid food processor begin processing the cucumbers, yogurt, mint and honey.
Once thoroughly blended pour into a bowl and place into the refrigerator for at least an hour.

Serve with a few mint leaves.

Cool and refreshing!

Soups, Stews and Chili

Notes:

64

D

DRY RUBBED RIBS

Chefs Notes: Loosen a corner of the membrane with a paring knife and with a small towel, grab the membrane and pull it diagonally across the ribs to remove it. Some scraping of the ribs may be required but this step is important to let the flavors of the dry rub contact the meat and make the ribs tenderer, yes, tenderer.

1 slab Pork ribs - pull the membrane from the rib side-See Chefs Notes.
1/2 cup Chef and the Fatman Love Rub or alternate ingredients below for rub
3 tablespoons Chili Powder
2 tablespoons Cumin
2 tablespoons kosher Salt
2 tablespoons Pepper
1 tablespoon Cayenne

Preheat BGE or oven to 350 degrees.

Place 2 handfuls of dry Jack Daniels chips in the bottom of the Egg just before grilling.

Wash and pat dry your ribs.

Make sure that the membrane on the non-meaty side is pulled off (see Chefs Notes).

Mix dry ingredients together in a separate bowl, or use Chef and the Fatman Love Rub, and rub all over the ribs.

Place in a big Ziploc bag and let them marinate for at least 2 days.

Grill until you ribs are juuuuust right.

Meats

Notes:

DUBLIN STYLE CORNED BEEF

What's a great cook book without a great Irish recipe?

5 pounds Corned Beef brisket
1 large Onion with
6 cloves Garlic embedded
6 peeled and sliced Carrots
8 new Potatoes, peeled and cubed
1 teaspoon Thyme, dried
1 bunch flat leaf Parsley
2 heads Cabbage, quartered
Sauce:
1/2 pint sour Cream
3 tablespoons Horseradish, prepared

Boil the beef, onion, carrots, potatoes, thyme and parsley in a pot
of water.
Simmer and cook for 3 hours.
Skim sediment and take out the thyme, parsley and onion.
Add the cabbage and simmer for a further 20 minutes or until the cabbage
is cooked.
Remove the meat and divide into pieces.
Remove and season the cabbage heavily with black pepper (or hot sauce to
taste).
On a large plate surround the beef with the cabbage, carrots and potatoes.
Prepare the horseradish sauce by whipping the cream and adding to the
horseradish.

Meats

Notes:

E

ESCAROLE SOUP

8 ounces ground Beef
1 pound parmesan Cheese, grated
1 slice stale Bread, pulsed in food processor until formed into rough breadcrumbs
1 teaspoon flat leaf Parsley
Salt and Pepper to taste
Combine all the ingredients above and form into balls, 1 inch in diameter
Set aside.
Soup:
4 cups Chicken Stock
1 head Escarole, cut into small pieces
1 small Onion
1/2 cup orzo Pasta
2 Eggs
2 tablespoons parmesan Cheese
Salt to taste

Bring broth to a boil in a large saucepan.

Add the escarole, onion, and meatballs.

Cook about 3 minutes.

Add the Orzo and cook 4-5 minutes.

In a bowl, whisk together the eggs and parmesan cheese.

Reduce the heat on the soup and whisk in the egg mixture.

Cook 2 more minutes.

Serve hot (approximately 150 degrees).

Soups, Stews and Chili

Notes:

F

FISH TACOS

1 1/2 pound Fish fillets (Orange Roughy, Grouper, or Snapper)
Salt and Pepper
1 tablespoon Lime juice
package Lettuce, large leaf
1 Jalapeno, minced
1 cup Cilantro, chopped
3 tablespoons grainy Mustard
1/3 cup extra virgin olive Oil Soft
Taco or Burrito shell

Preheat BGE to 350 degrees.

Season the fish filets with salt and pepper.

Grill or pan sauté the fish.

In a mixing bowl combine the jalapeno, mustard, cilantro and lime juice.
Slowly drizzle in the oil.

On a soft taco or burrito shell, arrange a lettuce leaf then place some fish on the lettuce.

Top with the sauce.

Roll like a burrito and chow down.

Seafood

Notes:

FISH TEQUILA TACOS

Remember use good tequila that you would serve a guest. Heck, taste it first just to make sure it's right.

1 pound mild white Fish (Mahi Basa, Perch, but not Flounder-it is too delicate)
5 Limes
1/2 cup Jicama, julienned
1/2 cup Carrots, shredded
1/2 cup Queso Blanco, shredded
1 Jalapeno, sliced
1 ounce Tequila
Soft Taco shells

Preheat grill or BGE to 350 degrees.
In a Ziploc bag, mix the juice from 3 limes and the Tequila.
Add the fish and marinate for 1 hour in the refrigerator.
Using a wok basket for the grill, remove the fish from the bag and cook until done.
Discard the marinade.
Marinate the jicama and carrots in juice from remaining limes and salt & pepper.
Remove fish from grill and let it rest.
Assemble the tacos by placing the fish on ½ of the soft taco shell.
Top with jicama/carrot mixture, add cheese.
Fold in half and enjoy!

Seafood

Notes:

FIVE SPICE CRUSTED SALMON

1/4 cup Coriander seeds
1/4 cup Cumin seeds
1/4 cup Fennel seeds
1/4 cup white Peppercorns
1/4 cup black Peppercorns
4 pieces Salmon about 6-8 oz each
1/4 cup canola Oil

Lightly crush the seeds and peppercorns to open up the oils in the seeds.
Wet the skin side of the salmon with water and dredge the skin in the spice mix.
Heat about 1/4 cup of oil in a large skillet on medium high.
Place the salmon in the pan skin side down and cover.
Cook for about 6-7 minutes do not flip.
Serving suggestion: Serve over steamed cabbage and bacon.

Seafood

Notes:

FLAN

1 1/2 cups Sugar
1 cup Water
2 cups Milk
2 cups Half and Half
8 Eggs
4 Egg yolks
3/4 cup Sugar
1 Vanilla Bean, split and scraped

Preheat oven to 325 degrees.

Make a caramel by combining 1 1/2 cups sugar with water in a medium saucepan.
Cook for about 15 minutes until it turns amber brown.
Carefully pour caramel into a 9-inch casserole dish then gently swirl to coat sides just a little bit. Set aside.

Heat the milk and Half and Half with the vanilla bean added.

Bring to a boil.

In another bowl whisk the eggs and egg yolks with the 3/4 cup sugar.

Slowly add the hot milk into the eggs, tempering the mixture. Keep whisking so the eggs don't scramble.
Once the egg mixture is warm, remove the vanilla bean.

Pour into the caramel coated casserole dish.

Place the flan into a bigger baking dish and add enough water around it to make a water bath.

Bake for about 45 - 50 minutes. Remove and let sit at room temperature for about an hour. Move to refrigerator for about 6 hours or overnight.
Run a knife around edge, cover with a plate, invert and serve.

Desserts

Notes:

FLOURLESS CHOCOLATE CAKE

4 ounces Butter, unsalted
8 ounces unsweetened Chocolate
5 Eggs, separated
2/3 cup Sugar

Preheat the oven to 350 degrees.

Butter and flour a 10-inch round cake pan.

Combine the butter and the chocolate in a double boiler over medium low heat (the water in the pot should not touch the bottom of the top bowl in your double boiler) melt chocolate.

Whisk together the egg yolks and melted chocolate.

Using a stand mixer (Kitchen Aid) beat the egg whites until they form soft peaks.

While the mixer is running slowly add the sugar until stiff peaks are formed.

Carefully, FOLD the chocolate into the beaten egg whites.

Pour into the prepared cake pan and bake 1 1/4 hours (check at 1 hour).

As the cake cools it will sink and crack. That is normal.

Top with favorite topping and enjoy.

Desserts

Notes:

FOUR BERRY COBBLER

BGE is the Big Green Egg. It is a ceramic cooking vessel that is VERY versatile.

1 pint Strawberries, halved
1 pint Blackberries
1 pint Raspberries
1 pint Blueberries
Juice of 1 Orange
Juice of 1 Lemon
2 tablespoons Grand Marnier
1/4 cup Sugar
5 tablespoons Cornstarch
2 teaspoons Cinnamon (optional)

Preheat BGE or oven to 350 degrees.

In a large mixing bowl, combine all ingredients except the streusel mix.

Let sit 5 - 10 minutes to marry the flavors.

In another bowl combine the butter, flour and sugar to create a streusel mix.

Place berry mixture in soufflé dishes and top with streusel mix.

Place in BGE or oven, bake for about 25 minutes, using indirect heat.

Serving Ideas: Serve with a great vanilla ice cream.

Desserts

Notes:

FRESH PASTA

With a Chef named Genovese, you just knew you had to have a homemade pasta recipe. It's quick and easy.

4 large Eggs
1 tablespoon Water
3 1/2 cups Flour, all-purpose, sifted
1/2 teaspoon Salt

Using a stand mixer, combine all ingredients and beat with flat beater for 30 seconds.
Switch to the dough hook and knead for 2 minutes.
Remove and divide into 8 pieces and work into pasta sheeter.
Cook pasta in rapidly boiling water until it is al dente - about 2-3 min.
Drain and serve.

Pasta

Notes:

FRIED GREEN TOMATOES

You can do the same recipe and leave off the egg; it's your choice.

4 green Tomatoes, sliced
Flour for dusting
2 Eggs
Cornmeal
Salt and Pepper to taste
Bacon grease or your favorite Oil

Slice tomatoes between ¼ to ½ inch thick.

Salt and pepper the tomato slices, dust lightly with flour.

Whisk eggs in a bowl and dip slices, letting the excess drip off.

Coat well with cornmeal (or bread crumbs).

Fry in hot grease or oil until browned, turning gently (approximately 3 minutes each side).

Veggies

Notes:

FUDGE TOPPED BROWNIES

1 cup Butter
4 ounces unsweetened Chocolate
2 cups Sugar
2 teaspoons Vanilla extract
4 Eggs
1 1/2 cups Flour, all-purpose
1 teaspoon Baking Powder
1/2 teaspoon Salt
1 cup Walnuts, chopped
Whipped Topping
4 1/2 cups Sugar
1 can (12 oz) evaporated Milk
1 cup Butter
1 package (12 oz) semisweet Chocolate chips
1 package (12 oz) milk Chocolate chips
1 jar (7 oz) Marshmallow Cream
2 teaspoons Vanilla extract
2 cups Walnuts, chopped

Preheat oven to 350 degrees.

For Brownie:

In a saucepan over low heat, melt butter and chocolate. Remove from heat.

Blend in sugar and vanilla. Beat in eggs.

Combine flour, baking powder and salt. Add to chocolate mixture. Stir in nuts.

Pour into a greased 13x9x2-inch baking pan.

Bake for 25-30 minutes or until top springs back when lightly touched.

For Topping:

In a heavy saucepan combine sugar, milk and butter. Bring to a boil over medium heat.

Reduce heat. Simmer 5 minutes, stirring constantly. Remove from heat.

Stir in the chips, cream, and, vanilla. Beat until smooth.

Add nuts. Spread over warm brownies.

Freeze until firm. Cut into 1-in squares.

Store in the refrigerator.

Desserts

G

GEORGIA WILD SHRIMP PO BOY

WOW what a lunch!!!!!

4 tablespoon Butter
Extra virgin olive Oil
Garlic, minced
1 pinch Cayenne pepper
1/4 cup white Wine
Juice from 1/2 Lemon
1/2 teaspoon Worcestershire sauce
1/2 teaspoon Lemon zest, finely chopped
1 1/2 pound Wild Georgia Shrimp, peeled and deveined
4 Hoagie Rolls

In a large sauté pan, combine butter and oil. Heat until butter is melted.
Add garlic and Cayenne pepper to taste. Cook until garlic is soft but not browned.
Add wine, and bring to a boil.
Lower the heat and add remaining ingredients, except bread.
Stir until the shrimp begins to turn pink.
Cut the hoagie bread open and place in a large bowl.
Spoon in the shrimp, and add a little sauce.

Seafood

Notes:

GOAT CHEESE STUFFED SOURDOUGH BREAD

1 loaf of sourdough Bread, sliced and buttered
1 log Goat Cheese, plain or herb
2 Eggs, beaten lightly with a splash of Water

In a small bowl mix the eggs and a few drops of water.
Spread goat cheese on each slice of bread.
Dip the bread into the egg mixture like you would french toast.
Melt the butter in a skillet over medium heat.
Cook on each side about 3 minutes.
Cut the bread into 2 triangles and serve.

Appetizers

Notes:

GORILLA BREAD

This is another goodie that can be an appetizer or a meal. Lots of calories...remember moderation.

1/2 cup Sugar
2 teaspoon Cinnamon
1 stick Butter
1 cup brown Sugar
1 pack cream Cheese, room temperature
2 cans Refrigerated Biscuit Dough
1 1/2 cups Nuts, chopped (your choice)

Preheat BGE or oven to 350 degrees.

Spray a Bundt pan with a non-stick cooking spray.

Mix the cinnamon and sugar together and set aside.

In a small saucepan melt the butter and brown sugar together. Set aside.

Open both packs of the biscuits and press them out a little. Sprinkle them with the sugar/cinnamon mix.

In the center of each biscuit place a small amount of the cream cheese. Fold them over so they look like Ravioli.

 In the bottom of the Bundt pan, (which will become the top when you turn it over) place nuts.

Place 10 of the folded biscuits in the pan.

Pour 1/2 of the butter/brown sugar syrup on top of the biscuits.

Layer the rest of the biscuits on top.

Sprinkle with the sugar/cinnamon mix and top with syrup. Bake for 30 minutes and let cool for 5 minutes.

Place a plate on top and invert.

Get that cup of coffee and enjoy!

Appetizers

Notes:

GRAHAM CRACKER CRUST FROM SCRATCH

1 cup Graham Cracker crumbs, from about 15 graham crackers
1/2 cup Sugar
1/4 cup melted Butter

Preheat oven to 350 degrees.

Process crackers to right consistency (the size of coarse sand).

Put in bowl.

Add sugar and butter.

Mix well.

Firmly pack into pie shell. Can be cooked for 10 minutes or used as is.

Desserts

Notes:

GRANDMA STOCK'S TENDERLOIN WITH WHITE PEPPER GRAVY

Recipe provided by Chef Mike Stock's Grandma! This recipe performed and provided by CFM Executive Sous Chef Mike Stock at Poole's Bar-B-Q in East Ellijay, GA

1 1/2 pounds Pork Tenderloin cut into chunks
4 tablespoons Butter
4 tablespoons Flour
2 cups whole Milk, room temperature
Salt
Plenty of freshly ground black Pepper

Heat pan until fairly hot, drop in cubed butter and stir immediately, taking pan off from stove if butter starts to brown.

Add pork chunks. Turn heat to medium high and brown pork in the butter, turning when each side is browned.

Set pork aside but keep warm. Shake flour into pan (with a flour shaker), stirring with either a whisk or a wooden spoon to incorporate all of the "fond" (bits and bites of browned pork) on the bottom of the pan.

Shake in more flour until you think the butter will hold no more flour (about 3-4 Tbl.). Let the flour/butter mixture cook in the pan on medium heat until the flour taste is cooked away but the roux has not browned.

Add some of the milk, whisking quickly to incorporate.

Allow the mixture to come to temperature and add more milk, adjusting until the right (slightly thin) consistency is reached.

Add salt and pepper.

Add back the pork.

Cook for a minute or two until the pork is warm enough and the sauce is just right!

Meats

Notes:

GREEK ISLES MARINADED CHICKEN

Recipe provided by Anthony C. Seta, C.M.C.

3 Chickens, halved
3 tablespoons lemon Pepper
2 teaspoons Durkees Chicken Seasoning
2 teaspoons Montreal Steak Seasoning
Lemon zest from 2 Lemons
1 cup Lemon juice
1 tablespoon Oregano, dried
3/4 cup vegetable Oil

Preheat oven to 375 degrees.

Combine all ingredients & blend well.

Separate the breasts from the thighs and legs. Place in a 2-gallon Ziploc bag.

Cover the Chicken with the marinade.

Turn bag 2-3 times when marinating.

Marinate for a minimum of 2 hours-maximum 24 hours.

Line a sheet pan with parchment paper. Arrange the chicken on the parchment covered sheet pan.

Place the sheet pan of marinated chicken in oven for 30-40 minutes.

Chicken must be golden brown with a 165F internal temperature.

Arrange the golden brown chicken on a platter or portion on an individual plate and spoon the pan drippings over the chicken.

Sauces/ Dressings and Gravies/Poultry

Notes:

GRILLED CHICKEN WITH SMOKED MUSHROOMS

1 Chicken breast, per person
1/3 pound Mushrooms, per person
Olive Oil
Balsamic Vinegar
Salt and Pepper to taste
1 pound your favorite Pasta

Preheat BGE or oven to 400 degrees.

Add some of your favorite smoking chips.

Smoke the mushrooms for about 15 minutes so they absorb a deep smoke flavor.

Grill the breasts with only salt and pepper.

Cook the pasta per directions.

When chicken is done remove it from the BGE or grill and let it rest for 5 minutes.

In a large bowl, mix the pasta with a little olive oil (not extra virgin).

Cut the mushrooms to bite size, along with the chicken.

Mix well and add a drizzle of Balsamic vinegar.

Season to taste.

Poultry

Notes:

GRILLED EGGPLANT POCKET

1 large Eggplant
1 log Goat Cheese
6 slices ham (prosciutto works best)
12 leaves Basil, fresh Marinade
1/4 cup balsamic Vinegar
1/4 cup extra virgin olive Oil
3 cloves Garlic
Salt and Pepper

Preheat the BGE to 350 degrees.

Combine all the marinade ingredients in a bowl.

Cut the eggplant lengthwise into 6 pieces.

Marinate the eggplant about 20 minutes before placing on the grill.

Grill eggplant until done, about 4 minutes a side. Let cool slightly.

Lay the eggplant down and smear the goat cheese over the eggplant. Top it with the ham and basil.

Roll up and slice on the bias.

Veggies

Notes:

GRILLED SHRIMP TOAST

1 pound Shrimp(Wild Georgia Shrimp), peeled and deveined
1/4 cup green Onions, chopped
1 small Jalapeno, minced
1/2 cup heavy Cream
4 ounces cream Cheese
1/2 bunch Cilantro
White crustless Bread
1 Egg white

Preheat BGE or Toaster Oven to 250.

In the bowl of a food processor mix raw shrimp, green onions, cilantro, jalapeno, egg white until smooth.
Fold in the cream cheese.
Spread mixture on both sides of the bread. Crimp the edges and cook on the BGE or toaster oven at 250, until golden brown.
Cut and enjoy.

Seafood

Notes:

H

HARVEST TOMATO VINAIGRETTE

Recipe provided by Chef Fred's wife Linda.

1 can Campbell's Tomato Soup
1 teaspoon Dijon mustard
3/4 cup apple cider Vinegar
1 teaspoon Salt
3/4 cup Sugar
Pepper to taste
1 tablespoon red Onion, chopped
1 tablespoon Hot Sauce
1 1/2 cups canola Oil

Place all ingredients (except oil) into a food processor (or blender).

While running at high speed, add the oil in a slow steady stream.

Toss with your favorite salad, sliced cucumbers, diced green bell pepper, sliced tomatoes and/or sliced red onion.

Sauces/ Dressings and Gravies

Notes:

HOMEMADE BBQ SAUCE

2 Shallots, minced
1 cup Tomato puree
1 cup Tomato, peeled and chopped
1/4 cup apple cider Vinegar
1 tablespoon Worcestershire sauce
1/4 cup brown Sugar
Chili Powder to taste

In a medium size saucepan, combine all ingredients.
Cook over a medium low heat for about 15 minutes.
If a smoother sauce is desired, place in a blender or food processor.
Adjust seasoning, as you like.

Sauces/ Dressings and Gravies

Notes:

HORIATIKI SALATA (GREEK PEASANT SALAD)

This recipe is from Athena George Penson, CPC (a certified personal chef) and great friend. This is the real deal for Greek Salad lover's baby.

1 head romaine Lettuce
1 pint grape Tomatoes
1 Cucumber, peeled, leaving a few strips of green skin on
1 green Pepper, cut into rings (optional)
1 small red Onion, sliced in thin rings
1 tablespoon Capers (more if you like)
4 pepperocini Peppers (optional)
1/4 cup Feta Cheese, crumbled (to taste)
Kalamata Olives, (to taste)
2 Anchovies, (optional)
Radishes (optional)
4 Eggs, hard-boiled, cut in quarters
For a vinaigrette dressing:
5 1/2 teaspoons Dijon mustard
3 part extra virgin olive Oil (to taste) (tradition is to just use good quality olive Oil and red wine vinegar for dressing)
1 part red wine Vinegar (to taste)
1teaspoon Salt, Pepper, Oregano (to taste)
2 cloves of Garlic, smashed and minced
A platter to arrange and serve salad on

Wash vegetables and set aside to drain. Make the dressing, refrigerate.

Cut vegetables to bite size.

Arrange everything nicely on the platter, except for the eggs and anchovies. They will go on the top of the salad.
Pour the dressing over the salad and serve.

Salads

Notes:

93

HORSERADISH AND BLEU CHEESE ENCRUSTED RIB EYE

1 large Rib eye, about 14 oz
1 jar Horseradish
6 ounces bleu Cheese

Preheat BGE or oven to 450 degrees.

Drain the horseradish.

Season steak with salt and pepper.

Bring to room temperature.

Grill steak until it is 3/4 cooked.

Remove and top with the drained horseradish and bleu cheese.

Place back on the grill (cheese side up) and let the cheese turn golden brown and bubbly.

Remove form the grill and let it rest.

Meats

Notes:

HORSERADISH MASHED POTATOES WITH CARAMELIZED ONIONS

1/4 cup Butter plus 6 tablespoons Butter
2 1/4 pounds Vidalia Onions, thinly sliced
3 tablespoons balsamic Vinegar
2 tablespoons Thyme, fresh chopped
1/2 pounds russet Potato, peeled
6 tablespoons whole Milk
1/4 cup Horseradish

Preheat BGE or oven to 350 degrees.

Melt 1/4 cup butter in large skillet over medium heat.

Add onions; sauté until deep golden, about 30 minutes.

Add vinegar and thyme.

Reduce heat to low.

Season with salt and pepper.

Meanwhile, cook potatoes in large pot of boiling salted water until very tender, about 20 minutes. Drain.

Return to same pot; mash until smooth.

Add 6 tablespoons milk, horseradish and 6 tablespoons butter; stir to blend. Thin with 2 tablespoons milk if necessary.

Season with salt and pepper.

Transfer potatoes to serving dish.

Spoon onion mixture atop potatoes.

Or add a portion of onions and stir them in. (Can be prepared 8 hours ahead).

Cover with foil and refrigerate.

Reheat in BGE for about 30 minutes before serving.

Serve hot.

Veggies

HOT CHEESY BEEF DIP

Serve in decorative casserole dish or in the two ramekins. Chef's Choice would be to prepare two ramekins. Heat one to serve when guests arrive, and then heat another a little later so that late arriving guests can also have some of this delicious beef dip.

2 jars (8 oz) dried Chipped Beef
1 small green bell Pepper, finely chopped
1 small Onion, finely chopped
2 packages (8 oz ea) cream Cheese, room temperature
1 package (8 oz) cheddar Cheese, shredded

Preheat BGE or oven to 350 degrees.

Rinse chipped beef in a bowl of water and drain and pat dry.
Chop the beef (if not chopped) into bite size or julienne strips.
Blend the cream cheese until soft and buttery in a Kitchen-Aid mixer using the flat blade.
Add the dried chipped beef, green bell pepper, onion, & cheddar cheese.
Mix for several minutes to completely incorporate all ingredients.
Spoon mixture into two small oven-proof dishes or Ramekins that have been sprayed with cooking spray, or into a buttered 3/4 qt. casserole dish.
Bake uncovered 30 - 45 minutes in the preheated oven, or until center is bubbly and edges are lightly browned.

Appetizers

Notes:

HOT CRAB DIP

3/4 cup cream Cheese
1 cup Mayonnaise
15 ounces canned Crabmeat
1/2 cup Onion, minced
2 tablespoons Lemon juice
1 teaspoon Hot Sauce

Preheat BGE or oven to 350 degrees.

Beat cream cheese and mayonnaise until smooth.

Stir in the crabmeat, minced onion, lemon juice and Texas Pete or your favorite hot sauce.

Spoon mixture into a small ovenproof dish that has been sprayed with cooking spray.

Place in over for 20 minutes or until the sauce is bubbly.

Serve with crackers, potato chips or tortilla chips.

You can also use fresh crabmeat in place of the canned crabmeat.

Appetizers

Notes:

HOT PEPPER SAUCE

1 cup Water
1/3 cup red wine Vinegar
1 hot Pepper (1-3 depending on how hot you want it!)
1 large red bell Pepper, chopped
1 small Onion, chopped
2 cloves Garlic, chopped
1 tablespoon Paprika
1 teaspoon Cumin
1 teaspoon Salt

Chop the pepper, onion, and, garlic.
Bring all the ingredients to a boil and simmer for eight minutes.
Allow it to cool somewhat and then puree in a blender.
Eliminate the hot peppers if you want a mild sauce.
Use jalapenos for hot, or, habaneras for a very hot sauce.

Sauces/ Dressings and Gravies

Notes:

I

ITALIAN POLENTA

Serve this corn grit instead of Mashed potatoes.

1 package Polenta
2 large spanish Onions
Butter

For temperature to cook see box instructions.

In a deep stockpot begin caramelize the onions.

This can take 10-15 minutes; take your time to accomplish this step.

When the onions are a dark earthy sweet brown add the amount of water or stock you will need to make the correct amount of Polenta.

When polenta is cooked (according to box instructions), transfer it to another bowl or cutting board to cut.

Veggies

Notes:

ITALIAN SAUSAGE BURGERS

5 pound Pork Butt cleaned of any silver skin and very little fat
1 teaspoon Cayenne (if you like it hot)
Salt & Pepper to taste
1 teaspoon Fennel seeds
1 clove Garlic, minced
1 medium Onion, finely chopped

Preheat BGE to 600 degrees.

In a meat grinder grind the meat twice.

Add all the seasoning and work in a mixing bowl.

Let rest in refrigerator overnight to let flavors blend, then form into patties.

Grill approximately 5 minutes a side, to a medium well done stage.

Meats

Notes:

ITALIAN SAUSAGE STUFFED BELL PEPPERS

3 green bell Peppers
1 pound ground Beef or Italian Sausage (or combination of the two)
1/4 cup Onion, chopped
1/4 cup Celery, chopped
8 oz Tomato sauce
1 teaspoon of Baking Soda
Salt and Pepper to taste
1/2 cup cooked Rice or Pasta (optional)

Preheat BGE or oven to 350 degrees.

Cut the tops off the peppers and clean out the insides.

Bring a big pot of water to boiling and add salt and 1 teaspoon of baking soda per gallon of water (the salt is for taste and the baking soda is to keep the peppers green).

Cook the peppers about 5 minutes and remove to let cool.

In the meantime, begin to sauté the onions and celery with a little olive oil.

Then add the ground beef and/or the sausage.

Drain the fat and return to the sauté pan.

Add the tomato sauce and pasta/rice.

Check for seasoning.

Remove from heat and cool.

Stuff your peppers and place in an ovenproof dish.

Bake for about 25 minutes and serve.

Meats

Notes:

ITALIAN SAUSAGE WITH PASTA

1 pound mild or hot Italian Sausage
1 red bell Pepper
1 green bell Pepper
1/2 pound shitake or exotic Mushroom
1 pound angel hair Pasta
1 cup your favorite Tomato sauce

In a medium high skillet heat sausage that has been sliced into 1 inch slices.
Cook for about 7-9 minutes or until done.
Remove sausage and begin to sauté the sliced pepper.
Season the peppers with salt and pepper.
While the peppers sauté begin boiling water for the pasta.
Don't forget to salt and oil the water.
When the water comes to a rolling hard boil add the pasta and cook until al dente.
Add the sauce to the peppers and heat through.
Drain pasta and pour into a large bowl.
Place the sauce and peppers on top of pasta, along with the sausage.

Meats

Notes:

K

KAREN'S "FLYING D" CHILI FROM TEDS MONTANA GRILL

This comes from a hugely popular bison restaurant that was started in Atlanta, Ted's Montana Grill. Check one out if you are ever around one. It is delicious, fun and very tasty. Bison doesn't have to be dry and wild tasting.

2 1/2 pounds fresh ground Bison
1/4 cup vegetable Oil
1 cup Onion, diced fine
1 clove Garlic, chopped fine
1 quart Water
3 tablespoons Beef Base
1 cup Tomato paste
1 1/2 teaspoons Salt
1 teaspoon Oregano leaves
1/4 teaspoon Cayenne pepper
1/2 teaspoon lack Pepper
1 1/2 teaspoons Sugar
1 1/2 teaspoons ground Cumin
3 tablespoons Chili powder
1 cup stewed Tomatoes
1 cup ranch style Beans

Heat oil and add the meat, breaking up any large chunks.

When the meat is half way cooked, add the onion and garlic.

Sauté until soft.

Add water, beef base, and tomato paste. Bring to a boil.

Add seasonings and simmer for 10 minutes.

Add beans and stewed tomatoes.

Cook for one additional minute.

Meats, Soups, Stews and Chili

Notes:

KD'S BITTERSWEET CHOCOLATE MOUSSE

When you're craving something really "bad" for you, this creamy, rich dark chocolate mousse hits the spot. It's made without egg yolks, butter, or heavy cream. It's definitely a once-in-awhile treat, but it's worth saving up for. Prepared, provided and performed by Chef Kathleen Daelemans and Vanessa Parker on Chef and the Fatman at Macy's in Atlanta.

4 ounces bittersweet Chocolate, chopped
2 tablespoons grape seed or canola Oil
2 teaspoons instant Coffee dissolved in hot water below
1 teaspoon hot Water
6 large Egg whites
1/4 teaspoon Cream of Tartar
2 tablespoons Sugar

Place chocolate in a large microwave-safe bowl and melt on medium-low, about 2 minutes.
Whisk in oil and coffee and blend until smooth. Set aside.

In a large bowl with an electric mixer, beat egg whites and cream of tartar on medium speed.

Gradually add sugar and continue beating until you have soft peaks.

Fold one fourth of the chocolate mixture into egg whites, then fold egg white mixture into remaining chocolate mixture and stir until completely incorporated.
Divide among dessert dishes and chill for 1 hour before serving.

Desserts

Notes:

KD'S STEAMED ASPARAGUS WITH LEMON, OLIVE OIL & PARMESAN

Recipe provided and prepared by Chef Kathleen Daelemans with her assistant Vanessa Parker and performed on Chef and the Fatman at Macy's in Atlanta.

1 bunch Asparagus, stems trimmed
Juice of one Lemon
Coarse Salt and cracked black Pepper
2 teaspoons extra virgin olive Oil
Parmesano Reggiano Cheese

Steam asparagus.

Place in large salad bowl.

Add lemon, salt and pepper to taste and olive oil.

Toss to coat well.

Taste and adjust seasonings.

Divide among salad plates.

Using a carrot peeler, shave off paper-thin slices of Parmesan over each salad.

Serve immediately.

Veggies

Notes:

KEY WEST BBQ SAUCE

2 cups packed brown Sugar
3 cups Ketchup
1 Lime, squeezed
2 navel Oranges, squeezed
1 Grapefruit, squeezed
1 Lemon, squeezed
1 cup Pineapple juice
1 cup Papaya juice

Mix all in a saucepan and bring to a simmer.
Adjust seasoning and apply to meat last 5 min.

Sauces/ Dressings and Gravies

Notes:

KIELBASA CHOWDER

1 pound Kielbasa, cut in 1/8" slices
1 medium Onion, chopped
4 Potatoes
2 cups salted Water
Salt and Pepper
1 small Cabbage, shredded
3 cups Milk
3 teaspoons Flour, stirred into milk above
1 cup cheddar Cheese, sharp, shredded
Pepper to taste

Boil 1st 4 ingredients and cook for 20 min.
Add cabbage, cook 10 minutes until tender.
Add milk/flour mixture, simmer 10 min.
Add cheese, and simmer 10 min.

Soups, Stews and Chili

Notes:

109

L

LAMB CHOPS

Dijon Mustard
Fresh Rosemary
Lamb Chops

Preheat BGE to 375 degrees.
Smear the chops with the mustard, coating completely.
Let rest with the mustard about 20 minutes at room temperature.
While the chops are resting, finely chop the fresh rosemary.
Sprinkle the mustard coated chops with the rosemary and again let rest about 20 minutes.
Grill until an internal temp of 140 (rare) and 145 (medium rare).
Remove from grill and rest before eating.

Meats

Notes:

LAYERED BLACK BEAN DIP

1 cup black Beans (canned are fine but rinse them a few times)
1 Jalapeno, chopped (optional)
1 Tomatoes, chopped and seeded
1 cup Cheddar cheese, grated
1 cup sour Cream
3 ripe Avocados, smashed into a guacamole mixture (add in some lemon juice as well)
1/4 bunch Cilantro, chopped

Mash the black beans to make a spread.
In a pie pan spread the black beans on the bottom.
Layer the remaining ingredients in order given and serve with tortilla chips.

Appetizers

Notes:

LEG OF LAMB

1 boneless leg of Lamb (you can get the whole leg and bone it out yourself)
3 tablespoons olive Oil
2-4 tablespoons Soy or Worcestershire sauce
4 cloves Garlic, sliced into 20 slivers
2 teaspoon Lemon juice
2 teaspoon fresh Rosemary

Preheat BGE or oven to 375 degrees.
Take your leg (lamb leg) and make little slits into the meat. Place slivers of garlic in the holes. Do this about 20 times at least.
Mix everything else together and pour into a Ziploc bag along with the meat and marinate for at least 2 hours.
Now Egg away until the internal temperature hits 140-145.
Let the Lamb REST at least 10 - 15 minutes before serving.

Meats

Notes:

LINDA'S POTATO SALAD

This recipe is from Chef Fred's wife Linda.

3 pounds small red bliss Potatoes, diced with skin on
1/2 cup finely chopped Onions or Scallions
2-3 stalks finely chopped Celery
2 boiled Eggs, chopped
3/4 cup real Mayonnaise
3 tablespoons sweet Pickle Relish
1 teaspoon Celery salt
1 teaspoon Garlic
salt Pepper to taste
pinch of Sugar

Boil the potatoes until fork tender.
Drain well and place in refrigerator until cool.
Peel and chop the eggs.
In a large mixing bowl combine all ingredients and adjust the seasoning.
Place salad back into the refrigerator for at least 3 hours.

Salads

Notes:

LOBSTER BISQUE

3 Live Maine Lobsters
6 cups salted Water
3 tablespoons Butter
2 Celery ribs
2 Leeks, washed and sliced
1 medium Onion, chopped
2 tablespoons Flour, all-purpose
1 1/4 cup heavy Cream

Bring salted water to a boil and then place lobsters in the water.
Cook for about 8-10 min.
Remove lobsters and allow cooling. Remove tail meat and place shells
back into water.
In another saucepan melt the butter and sauté the vegetables about 5
minutes.
Add the flour and continue to stir.
Strain the lobster stock into the vegetables and whisk until smooth.
Puree the soup and slowly bring soup back up to temp.
Slowly add the cream and garnish with chopped tail meat.

Soups, Stews and Chili

Notes:

LOBSTER PASTA

2 Live Maine lobsters
1 pound Pasta
16 ounces heavy Cream
1 pack sun dried Tomatoes
1 medium Onion
Old Bay Seasoning

In a large pot, put sufficient water to boil the Lobsters, and add quartered onion.

Add some old bay seasoning to taste.

As the water is boiling, say good-bye to your little friends (while the water is boiling, put them in the freezer for 1 hour if you want to be sure they don't feel anything- you softie)!

Add the lobsters to the boiling water and cook about 10 minutes.

Remove from the water but keep the water boiling (it is the water that we will cook the pasta in soon).

Add the tomatoes to a food processor and pulse to chop as smooth or chunky as you like.

Now add the cream to the tomatoes in the processor and combine. If the mixture gets too thick then add some lobster stock to thin it out a little bit.

Now remove the meat from the tail and claws and cut into bite size pieces.

Cook the pasta until "al dente".

Drain the pasta and toss with the sauce.

Sprinkle the pasta with the lobster and serve.

Pasta, Seafood

Notes:

LODGE CAST IRON BEEF STROGANOFF

1 medium Onion, diced
2 pounds lean ground Beef
Salt and Pepper to taste
1/3 teaspoon Garlic salt
1/3 teaspoon Celery salt
1 cup Water
24 ounces Tomato sauce
1 teaspoon Worcestershire sauce
1/2 cup sour Cream
1 bag (12 oz) egg Noodles

Brown the beef, onions, and, spices together in your Lodge cast iron dutch oven.

While the meat is browning, mix tomato sauce, Worcestershire sauce, and sour cream.

When meat is browned place uncooked noodles over the top and spread out.

Pour liquid mixture over the noodles. Cover and cook about 30 minutes until noodles are soft.

Meats

Notes:

LODGE PINEAPPLE UPSIDE DOWN CAKE

If you don't add cherries IMHO (in my humble opinion) it's not an official Pineapple Upside Down Cake.

1 1/4 cup cake Flour
1 1/4 teaspoon Baking Powder
1/4 teaspoon Salt
3/4 cup Sugar
4 tablespoons Butter
1/2 cup Milk
1 teaspoon Vanilla
1/2 cup brown Sugar
4 Pineapple rings in juice
4 tablespoons Butter
Cherries (optional to some…. not to us)

Preheat BGE or oven to 350 degrees.

Sift flour, salt, baking powder, and sugar into a bowl. Add 4 tablespoons butter, milk, and, vanilla.

In your cast iron skillet melt 4 tablespoons butter and brown sugar. When melted, add the pineapple slices.

Turn batter out on top of the pineapples and bake about 45 minutes (check at 30).

Loosen sides and invert onto a plate.

Add cherries if you like but not necessary

Desserts

Notes:

M

MAPLE BBQ CHICKEN WINGS

3 pounds Chicken wings or ribs
1 1/2 cups maple Syrup
2 tablespoons Chili Sauce
2 tablespoons Vinegar
1 1/2 tablespoons Onions, minced
1 tablespoon Worcestershire sauce
1 teaspoon Salt
1/2 teaspoon dry Mustard
1/8 teaspoon Pepper

Preheat BGE or oven to 350 degrees.
Mix all ingredients together except meat.
Brush both sides of meat with mixture.
Roast 1 1/2 hours.
Basting is optional.
Very sticky and very delicious.

Meats

Notes:

MARLBORO PIE

This is a traditional New England 18th Century Thanksgiving tradition. We hope you enjoy it.

24 ounce Applesauce, chunky, natural
1 2 tablespoons Butter, melted
1/2 cup Sugar
1 Lemon (to zest and for the juice)
2 Egg yolks
2 Eggs, whole
1/2 cup heavy Cream
1/3 cup Raisins
1/3 cup Walnuts
1- 9-inch deep dish Pie Crust

Pre-heat the oven to 350 degrees.

Reduce the applesauce in a saucepan over low heat until you have approximately 10 oz of applesauce.

Mix together 1 1/4 cup of applesauce, butter, and sugar.

Add the juice and zest of one lemon.

Beat the eggs with the cream.

Add to the apple mixture.

Place the raisins and walnuts in the pie shell.

Top with the mixture.

Bake for 25 - 35 minutes or until the pie is firm and the crust is lightly browned.

Let this pie stand and set up for at least 2 hours in refrigerator.

Bring out and let pie come to room temperature before serving.

Desserts

Notes:

MARVIN WOODS' FRENCH ONION SOUP

4 tablespoons Butter, unsalted
2 pounds yellow Onions, sliced
1/4-inch into half circles
2 Leeks, sliced in to half moons and rinsed
1 Shallot, chopped
1 teaspoon Sugar
1 tablespoon Flour, all-purpose
1/2 cups dry Sherry
1 1/2 quarts Beef Stock, preferably homemade
1 tablespoon Thyme, fresh, chopped
Coarse Salt and freshly ground black Pepper
1 small french Baguette, sliced crosswise into 1/2-inch pieces
8 ounces gruyère Cheese, grated on a box grater
Freshly snipped Chives for garnish

Melt butter in a large heavy-duty pot over medium-low heat.

Add onions, leeks, and shallots.

Season with salt and pepper.

Sprinkle with sugar, and cook, stirring just as needed to keep onions from sticking, until they are melting and soft, golden brown, and beginning to caramelize, 30 to 45 minutes.

Sprinkle flour over onions, and stir to coat.

Add sherry, stock, and thyme, and bring to a boil.

Reduce heat to simmer and cook, partially covered, for about 30 minutes.

Taste and adjust for seasoning with salt and pepper.

Ladle hot soup into six ovenproof bowls.

Arrange the bowls on a baking sheet.

Place 1 or 2 slices of baguette over each bowl of soup.

Sprinkle 1/2 cup grated cheese over baguette in each bowl, and place under the broiler until cheese is melted and crusty brown around the edges. Watch carefully that bread doesn't burn.

Garnish with freshly snipped chives.

Serve immediately.

Soups, Stews and Chili

MEXICAN CHOCOLATE FONDUE

12 ounces heavy whipping Cream
16 ounces semi-sweet Chocolate
4 Cinnamon sticks
1 teaspoon ancho Chili Powder

In medium saucepan bring the cream up to a low boil, add the cinnamon sticks.

Remove from the heat and steep for about 20 minutes.

Meanwhile place the semi-sweet chocolate and chili powder in a large mixing bowl.

Place the cream back on the stove and reheat to a medium boil (be careful it doesn't boil over).

Remove the cinnamon and pour the cream over the chocolate pepper combo.

Cover with plastic wrap and let sit for 5 minutes.

Remove plastic and whisk until incorporated.

Serve warm with fresh fruit, cake or dried fruit.

Desserts

Notes:

MEXICAN CORNBREAD

This recipe comes from the vault of Ms. Ada Sanders...My mother-in-law. It's easy and tastes great.

2 packages Jiffy Cornbread mix
2 Eggs
1 cup sour Cream
1 can cream-style Corn
1 pound browned and drained ground Beef
1 Onion, chopped
12 oz cheddar Cheese, shredded
Chopped Jalapeno to taste

Preheat BGE or oven to 350 degrees.

Mix the first four ingredients together and put 1/3 in the bottom of a hot cast iron skillet.

Add ground meat, onion, cheese and peppers.

Put remainder of cornbread mix on top.

Bake for 50 - 60 minutes until top browns.

Appetizers

Notes:

N

NO BAKE CHERRY CHEESE CAKE

1 can sweetened condensed Milk
1/3 cup Lemon juice
1 package (8 oz) cream Cheese
1/4 teaspoon Vanilla
1 graham cracker Pie Crust, 9 inch
1 can Cherry pie filling

Blend sweetened condensed milk and cream cheese.
Gradually blend in lemon juice and vanilla.
Beat until firm.
Pour into piecrust.
Chill for 3 hours.
Chill cherry pie filling.
Add chilled cherry topping.

Desserts

Notes:

NOT YO' MAMA'S BANANA PUDDING

From Paula Deen's show Paula's Home Cooking. This is an awesome recipe. If you are a traditionalist like we are, you can use regular vanilla wafers instead of Chessmen cookies. You can also use your stand mixer instead of hand mixer. Just some thoughts.

2 bags Pepperidge Farm Chessmen Cookies
6-8 Bananas, sliced
2 cups Milk
1 box (5 oz) instant french vanilla Pudding
1 package (8 oz) cream Cheese, room temperature
1 can (14 oz) sweetened condensed Milk
1 container (12 oz) frozen Whipped Topping, thawed

Line the bottom of a 13 by 9 by 2-inch dish with 1 bag of cookies and layer bananas on top.
In a bowl, combine the milk and pudding mix and blend well, using a handheld electric mixer.
Using another bowl, combine the cream cheese and condensed milk together and mix until smooth.
Fold the whipped topping into the cream cheese mixture.

Add the cream cheese mixture to the pudding mixture and stir until well blended.

Pour the mixture over the cookies and bananas and cover with the remaining cookies.
Refrigerate until ready to serve.

Desserts

Notes:

127

O

OLD FASHIONED TEA CAKES

My mother-in-law Ms. Ada Sanders contributed this classic.

1 stick Butter
2 3/4 cups Sugar
2 1/4 cups Flour, self-rising
2 Eggs
2 tablespoons Milk
5 1/2 teaspoon Vanilla

Preheat oven to 375 degrees.
Mix all ingredients together.
By small spoonfuls, place on cookie sheet and mash very flat with fork (dipped in water).
Bake until light brown. These will be very crispy.

Desserts

Notes:

ONION BREAD

You may sauté your onions ahead of time if you wish.

1 1/2 cups Bisquick
1 cups sharp cheddar Cheese, grated
2 tablespoons Butter, melted
1 medium Vidalia Onion, sliced or diced
1/2 cup Milk
1 Egg, beaten

Preheat BGE or oven to 400 degrees.

Using your Kitchen Aid mixer combine the Bisquick, milk and egg.
Mix until combined and then add butter, onions and cheese.
Spoon all the dough into a Kitchen Aid round cake pan.
Bake for 15 minutes.
Pull the bread out and sprinkle on the rest of the cheese. Bake another 10 minutes.

Appetizers

Notes:

ORANGE TAFFY

This is great for kids (after it's cooled and ready to roll). When we performed this recipe the kids in the audience had a ball rolling and playing with the newly created taffy.

2 cups Sugar
2 cups light Corn Syrup
1 can (6 oz) frozen Orange Juice concentrate
1 pinch Salt
1 cup Half-and-half
2 cup Butter

In a heavy saucepan, combine first four ingredients.
Cook and stir over medium heat until sugar is dissolved.
Bring to a rapid boil and cook until a candy thermometer reads 245 degrees (firm- ball stage).
Add Half-and-Half and butter. Cook and stir until mixture reaches 245 degrees again.
Pour into a greased 5-in. x 10-in. x 1-in. pan. Cool.
When cool enough to handle, roll into 1-1/2 inch logs or 1-inch balls.
Wrap individually in foil or waxed paper; twist ends.

Desserts

Notes:

OYSTER STEW

3 dozen fresh shucked Oysters
1/2 gallon whole Milk
1 quart heavy Cream
1/2 pound Tasso (dry cured spicy ham)
2 yukon gold Potatoes, cubed
2 sticks Butter

In a large stockpot bring to a medium boil the milk, cream, and butter.
After the milk mixture cooks for about 5 min, add the potatoes.
Taste the stew and add salt and white pepper (fine grind) to taste.
After the potatoes are fork tender, add the drained oysters and 1/2 stick of butter.
Stir with a wooden spoon and adjust the seasoning.
Bring back to a medium boil until the edges of the oysters just start to curl.
Pour into a large bowl and serve with a warm loaf of sourdough bread.
Garnish with fresh chopped parsley.

Seafood

Notes:

P

PAELLA

1 pound Scallops (10 - 15 CT)
1 pound Chicken
1 pound Shrimp (10-15 CT)
1 pound Mussels (10-15)
1 pound Clams (10-15)
1 package valencia Rice (short grain)
2 cups chorizo Sausage
1 red bell Pepper
1 green bell Pepper
5 cups Chicken Stock
15 threads Saffron
1 medium Onion

In a large sauté skillet heat olive oil and begin to brown the chicken.
Remove the chicken when it is browned on both sides.
Add the chopped onion and sweat for about 3 minutes.
Add the rice into the onions and cook about 1 minute.
Next add the SAFFRON.
Immediately add the 5 cups of chicken stock.
Bring this mixture to a boil and then reduce the heat and simmer 10 minutes.
After 10 minutes remove the lid and arrange the chicken, seafood, and, sausage.
Carefully add the peppers.
Replace lid and simmer about 10-15 minutes.
After the 10-15 minutes has expired open lid and let stand for 5 minutes.
Serve the Paella in the skillet.

Poultry, Seafood

Notes:

PAN SEARED VEAL CHOP & MUSHROOM CHIPOTLE CREAM SAUCE

These chops are best done on the BGE or on a hot grill. Pull the steaks off to rest when they are 133 degrees for rare (let them rest for a full 15 minutes)/142 degrees for medium (let them rest for a full 15 minutes), and don't buy good veal chops if you are going to cook them well done.

1 Veal chop per person (have your butcher "french" the bone)
Salt and Pepper
Chipotle Mushroom
Sauce ingredients below:
3 whole dried Chipotle peppers
12 ounces heavy whipping Cream
4 ounces Mushrooms, sliced

START WITH THE SAUCE:
In a heavy sauce pan add all ingredients (if you want more heat, chop one of the peppers. If not, just leave whole).
Slowly bring the mixture to a low boil and remove from the heat.

Let it rest for 30 minutes (this will help infuse the peppers earthy smoky flavor into both the cream and mushrooms).
When you are ready for the sauce remove the peppers and serve the sauce.
NOW TO THE CHOPS.

Remove from the refrigerator 20 minutes before you are going to cook them.

This step allows the meat to accept the seasoning.

Season the chops with salt and pepper.

Bring your skillet to a high temperature and add a little oil. Begin searing the chops.

If you wish, you can finish these chops in the oven to a temperature of about 145-150 when they are done, REST your meat.
Place chop on the plate and serve with the Chipotle cream sauce.

Meats

Notes:

PANKO DUSTED FRIED OYSTERS

1 dozen cleaned fresh Oysters
3 cups Panko breadcrumbs
4 large Eggs, beaten with 1 teaspoon of Water
6 cups vegetable Oil
Salt and Pepper

Heat oil to about 315-325 degrees.

Pick through your oysters and remove any shell fragments.

Beat the eggs and water to make an egg-wash.

Pour Panko breadcrumbs into another bowl next to the eggs.

Season both eggs and breadcrumbs with Salt and Pepper.

Put oysters in egg-wash, then into the breadcrumbs. Shake to remove the excess.

Slowly lower the breaded oysters into the oil.

Cook until they begin to float.

Remove with a slotted spoon and place onto paper towels to drain.

Season again with salt and pepper.

Serve with your favorite sauce.

Seafood

Notes:

PASTA CARBONARA

1 pound dry Pasta
2 tablespoons olive Oil
6 ounces Pancetta, diced
4 cloves Garlic, finely chopped
2 large Eggs
1 cup fresh grated parmesan Cheese

Prepare the sauce as you cook the pasta.

Heat the oil in a deep skillet over medium heat.

Add the pancetta and sauté for 3 minutes until crispy.

Toss in the garlic and cook about 30 seconds.

Add the drained pasta to the pan and toss.

Beat the eggs and cheese together in a mixing bowl.

Remove pan from heat and add the egg mixture into the pasta.

Toss quickly to keep the eggs from scrambling.

Thin the sauce a little if needed with the pasta water.

Pasta

Notes:

PASTITSIO

This should be prepared in a 13x9x2 pan. This one may take a little more time and effort but it will be worth it. From the kitchen of Athena George Penson, CPC.

Meat Sauce: 2 pounds ground Sirloin
1/2 pound ground Lamb
3 tablespoons olive Oil
1/4 cups Onion, finely chopped
3 cloves Garlic, minced
1 tablespoon Oregano, dried
1 bunch flat leaf Parsley, finely chopped
2 Bay Leaves (remove before building the pastitsio layers)
1 Cinnamon stick, whole
1 tablespoon Salt, to taste
2 tablespoons Pepper, to taste
1 cup red Wine, optional
2 tablespoons Tomato paste
1 can (15 oz) Tomato sauce
1 bullion cube of Chicken or half teaspoon Chicken base
half cup Water (more if sauce is too 'dry')
2 pounds dry Pasta (Penne or large spaghetti from Greek store)
Béchamel (Mornay) Sauce:
3/4 stick Butter, melt it in the heavy pot used to make béchamel in
1 quart Milk (maybe more)
1 1/2 cup all purpose Flour
1 cup plus...grated parmesan or Kefalotyri Cheese
1 dash or two of Nutmeg

Prepare meat sauce, a day ahead.

The next day...

Preheat oven to 350 degrees.

Boil pasta, just before preparing Béchamel.

Prepare a Béchamel Sauce combining 4 T butter, 1-cup milk, and 1/2 cup all-purpose flour, 1/2 cup grated parmesan and a pinch of nutmeg.

Assemble pastitsio.

Bake for approximately 45 minutes to an hour until golden on top.

Meats, Pasta

PEANUT BUTTER ICE CREAM TOPPING

1 cup packed brown Sugar
1/2 cup light Corn Syrup
3 tablespoons Butter
1 pinch Salt
1 cup creamy Peanut Butter
1/2 cup evaporated Milk
Vanilla Ice Cream
Peanuts, optional

Combine brown sugar, corn syrup, butter and salt in a pan.
Bring to a boil, stirring enough to keep anything from sticking to the bottom of the pan.
Add peanut butter; stir until smooth.

Stir in evaporated milk.

You may cover and store in the refrigerator.

Serve over good vanilla fleck ice cream and garnish with peanuts.

Desserts

Notes:

PICADILLO

1/4 cup olive Oil
2 pound lean ground Beef
1 small Onion, finely chopped
3 cloves Garlic, minced
3 ounces Tomato sauce
1 large Tomato, chopped
1 can (8 oz) green Olives (pimiento stuffed), sliced
1/2 cup burgundy Wine
1/2 tablespoon brown Sugar
3 grates of Nutmeg
1/4 cup Water, you may or may not need it
1 cup Raisins, optional

Use a large skillet with a tight fitting lid.
Add the oil to the pan and begin to cook the ground beef.
Season the beef with salt and pepper.
Cook until there is no pink left.
Remove meat and begin sweating the onion with the tomato.
Add meat back into the skillet and add the remaining ingredients except the water. Stir well.
Add the water if too thick. Lower the heat to about medium low and cook with the lid on for about 20-25 minutes.
Meanwhile cook up some white rice. Serve the Picadillo over the rice.

Meats

Notes:

POACHED PEARS

4 Pears, ripe and firm
3 cups Champagne
1 cup Sugar
1 Vanilla Bean

Using a fruit corer, remove the seeds from the pear, going from bottom to top, but leaving the top intact.
In a large stockpot, add champagne and sugar and bring to medium heat.
Split the vanilla bean in half and remove the "caviar" (scrape out the insides of the bean).
Add the vanilla "caviar" to the champagne mix in the pot.
Add the pears and poach about 7-9 minutes until fork tender.
Serve warm.

Desserts

Notes:

POACHED SNAPPER WITH COCONUT SAUCE

2 fillets Snapper (any firm flesh fish will do)
1 1/2 cups Poaching Liquid = (1 cup clam juice and 1/2 cup white
wine)
1 can coconut Milk
2 packs Uncle Ben's Rice pilaf
Salt and Pepper to taste

In a sauce pan over medium heat begin reducing the coconut milk.

In a large sauté pan slowly bring up the temperature of your poaching liquid.

Do not boil the liquid.

Medium temperature at most.

Season the fillets with salt and pepper.

When the coconut sauce is almost ready, add the fish into the poaching liquid.

The fish will take 10 - 15 minutes to poach.

Take the rice and prepare according to instructions.

When the fish is done, carefully remove it from the poaching liquid.

Serve over rice and drizzle sauce over fish.

Seafood

Notes:

PORK LOIN WITH SPINACH AND ANDOUILLE SAUSAGE

The Food Safety and Inspection Service of the USDA recommends 160-degree internal temperature (throughout) as the minimum safe standard for cooking pork loins.

1 pound Pork loin
1 link andouille Sausage
1 bunch Spinach
Salt and Pepper to taste

Preheat your BGE or oven to 350 degrees.

Butterfly the pork loin so it is like a tri-fold wallet.

Season both sides of the pork loin.

Cover the pork with spinach. Top with the link of sausage and roll up tight.

Use butchers twine (ask meat manager for some) to tie up roll.

Place in oven on roasting rack, or BGE, and cook until an internal temperature of 155 is reached.

Let rest. Carry over cooking will bring the temperature up to 160-degrees. Slice and serve.

Meats

Notes:

PORK ROULADE

This recipe was provided and performed by Chef and the Fat Man Executive Sous Chef Mike Stock.

4 Six ounce boneless Pork Chop or thin sliced Pork tenderloin pounded thin
4 slices Ham, sandwich sliced
4 slices smoked gouda Cheese
4 whole green Bean or Asparagus spears, blanched
1 pinch Salt
1 pinch Pepper
1 pinch Herbs de Provence

Preheat BGE or oven to 250 degrees.
Lay pork cutlet flat. Cover with ham and cheese. Place the asparagus or green beans to one end of the pork. Dust with spices.
Beginning on the end with the asparagus, roll the pork tightly, secure with a toothpick.
Lightly dust the roulade with flour and sauté until lightly brown on all sides.
Remove from pan and place in BGE or oven until ready to plate.

Meats

Notes:

PORK TENDERLOIN WITH POMEGRANATE SAUCE AND BACON

To get the Earls from the Pomegranate make about 3-4 slices into the skin of the fruit and soak in cold water for about 15 - 20 minutes. Peel the skin and then remove the seeds (earls) and discard the white pithy membrane.

2 whole Pork tenderloins
Earls from 2 whole Pomegranates
8 ounces Pomegranate juice
1/2 pound Bacon
Salt and Pepper to taste

In a medium high heated skillet, begin rendering the bacon.

Once the bacon is done remove from the pan and drain.

Remove almost all the grease from the pan and crank up the heat.

Once hot, begin to sear off the pork.

Once the pork is nice and brown remove the pork and add the Pom (pomegranate) juice and the "earls" of the fruit.

Add the pork back into the pan and cook until the pork is done (145 degrees).

Remove the pork and let it rest.

Continue to cook sauce until thickened and add crumbled bacon. (A slurry of 3 tablespoons chicken stock and 1 teaspoon cornstarch can be used as a thickening agent).

Slice the rested pork and top with the sauce.

Meats

Notes:

145

POTATO AND MUSHROOM GRATIN

3 pounds yukon gold Potatoes, peeled and sliced thinly
2 pounds large button Mushrooms
1/2 pint Whipping Cream
1 1/2 cups Cheese such as smoked gouda

Preheat BGE or oven to 350 degrees.

Butter a 3-quart casserole dish and begin layering the potatoes.

Add mushrooms and then cheese.

Repeat until about 1/2 inch from the top.
Season and slowly add 1/2 the cream, pushing down on the potatoes so the cream is dispersed throughout; add rest of cream same way.
Bake for 45-50 minutes uncovered.

Veggies

Notes:

POTATO CHIP CHICKEN

This recipe is one of the most requested and very popular with young and less young alike. Vary the chips for your own unique tastes.

1 big bag Sour Cream and Onion Chips
2 large Eggs, lightly beaten
1 pound Chicken breast, no skin, no bone, cut in strips or diced

Preheat oven to 350 degrees.

Open the bag of chips on one end and crush chips into small pieces.

Put the crushed chips in a bowl.

Put the chicken into the egg mixture and then roll into the chips.

Place on a baking sheet and bake for 15 minutes.

Serve with your favorite sauces.

Meats

Notes:

147

POTATO ENCRUSTED SEA BASS

1 filet per person Sea Bass
1 russet Potato, sliced thin with skin on
Salt and Pepper

Preheat BGE or oven to 350 degrees.
Slice the potato (skin on) and shingle on the filet.
In a medium high heat skillet, which has been oiled lightly, gently and carefully, place the filet in the pan.
Place with the potato side down. Turn carefully after 1 1/2 minutes.
Finish the fish in the oven for 8 -10 min.

Seafood

Notes:

POTATO PORK SKILLET

This fine recipe performed by Chef Mike Stock at Poole's Bar-B-Q in East Ellijay,
Georgia. The best-darned BBQ in North Georgia.

1 pound Pork Tenderloin, cut into 1/4 inch slices
2 tablespoons Butter
1 can chicken Stock, divided
8 small Potato, red, quartered
1 tablespoon Dijon mustard
2 teaspoons Worcestershire sauce
1/4 teaspoon Salt
1/2 teaspoon Pepper
1 cup fresh Mushrooms, sliced
1/2 cup green Onions, sliced
2 tablespoons Flour, all-purpose

In a large skillet over medium heat, brown pork in butter on both sides.
Remove and keep warm.

Set aside ¼ cup of broth.

Add the potatoes, mustard, Worcestershire sauce, salt, pepper, and,
remaining broth into the skillet.

Bring to a boil. Reduce heat; cover and simmer for 15-17 minutes or
until the potatoes are tender.

Stir in mushrooms, onions, and pork.

Cover and simmer 5 minutes longer or until meat is no longer pink. In
a small bowl combine the flour and reserved broth and stir until
smooth.

Stir broth into pork mixture. Bring to a boil; cook and stir for 2
minutes or until thickened.

Meats

Notes:

POTATO WRAPPED SALMON

4 ounces Salmon filets
6 ounces Dijon mustard
3 large Potatoes, white
Salt and Pepper to taste

Preheat oven to 350 degrees.
Peel the potatoes and place in a bowl of cold water.
This will help arrest the oxidation process.
When you have everything ready, grate the potatoes on a box grater using the large holes.
Take the salmon filets and spread them with the Dijon mustard, then season.
Roll filets in the grated potatoes.
Lay filets on a sheet of plastic wrap and wrap tightly. Refrigerate for 15 minutes in the refrigerator.
Heat a large skillet to medium high heat and then add a little olive oil.
Remove the filets from the wrap and begin searing the potatoes.
The potatoes will have lots of water in them. Oil and water don't mix, so it will spit and spatter. Use a splatter shield.
When brown on the bottom turn and finish in oven until done.

Seafood

Notes:

Q

QUICK MARINARA

If you wish to have a smoother sauce place some into your Kitchen Aid food processor and pulse until you get the consistency you want, but be careful (splashing)!

1 large Onion
6 plum Tomatoes, diced
Salt and Pepper
Fresh herbs (Basil, Oregano, Thyme), chopped to taste

In a 6 qt saucepan heat a little oil and begin sweating the onions.
Season the onions and cook about 7 - 10 minutes.
Add the tomatoes and stir in the herbs.
Cook about 15 - 20 minutes to evaporate the liquid.

Sauces/ Dressings and Gravies

Notes:

R

RASPBERRY CREME BRULE

48 Raspberries
2 1/2 cups heavy Cream
8 Egg yolks
1/3 cup Sugar
12 teaspoons Sugar for burning
1 pinch Salt

Preheat oven to 300 degrees.

Place 8 raspberries in 6 ramekins.

Bring cream to a simmer. In a separate bowl whisk the egg yolks with the 1/3 cup sugar.

Slowly add cream to eggs and whisk constantly so eggs don't scramble.

Divide each into the ramekins and set into a baking pan.

Add hot water to come up to about 1/2 way up (water bath).

Bake for about 35-45 minutes.

Let cool at room temperature, and then put into the refrigerator over-night.

Sprinkle the sugar on top and flash burn under the broiler or blowtorch.

Desserts

Notes:

RED EYE GRAVY

2 tablespoons Butter
1 small Onion, finely chopped
2 tablespoons Flour, all-purpose
3/4 cup strong Coffee
3/4 cup chicken Stock
1/4 cup heavy whipping Cream
Salt and Pepper to taste

Add the butter and onion to a large saucepan and cook until the onions are soft.
Add flour and stir well. Cook for 2 minutes.
Add coffee and stock. Whisk well to combine and allow the sauce to cook until thickened.
Add the cream and adjust seasoning.
Let cook 5 minutes after you add the cream.
Hope you have a few biscuits left for this gravy!

Sauces/ Dressings and Gravies

Notes:

ROASTED PEACH BRULE WITH WHITE PEPPER CREAM SAUCE AND CRUZAN RUM SYRUP

These recipes are from the Chefs Clinton Del Marcelle and Christopher Effa from the Mondo Mocha Café Doubletree Atlanta Northwest - Windy Hill, Marietta, GA.

4 fresh tree ripe Georgia Peaches
4 Egg yolks
2 tablespoons Cornstarch
1/4 cup powdered Sugar
1/4 cup heavy Cream
1 teaspoon Almond extract
2 teaspoon real Vanilla extract
3 teaspoon white Pepper
1/2 cup dark Rum
1/4 cup Molasses
1 pinch Nutmeg and Cinnamon

Combine egg yolks, heavy cream, cornstarch, vanilla, and sugar in a double boiler.

Beat over double boiler until thickened; then add white pepper and almond extract.

Heat a small sauté pan. Add 3 tablespoons whole butter.

Place a halved peach rubbed with brown sugar into the pan. When nicely browned, remove.

Repeat with other peach halves.

Add rum and molasses. Reduce until syrup like consistency.

Serve syrup over peaches in dessert bowl.

Desserts

Notes:

156

ROASTED PUMPKIN SOUP

Now this one takes a little more work. However, it's worth it. Different, unique, and flavorful. A great fall soup

1 medium Pumpkin
Salt and Pepper
3 cups chicken Stock
4 cloves Garlic
Cinnamon
Nutmeg

Preheat BGE or oven to 350 degrees.

Cut pumpkin in half and scoop out the seeds (save them).

Salt and pepper the inside of the pumpkin.

Place cut side down on baking sheet.

Rub skin with oil and bake until fork tender.

Take the seeds and wash them with water and season with salt.

Roast seeds for about 5 minutes and reserve as a garnish.

After the pumpkin is done, scoop out the meat and place in food processor.

Pulse until smooth.

Place in stockpot and add the chicken stock.

Add a pinch of cinnamon and nutmeg.

Bring to a simmer and adjust seasoning.

Add the garlic about 20 minutes before serving.

Finally, garnish with roasted seeds.

Soups, Stews and Chili

Notes:

157

S

SALMON BURGERS

I know this sounds strange but it's really simple and delicious. It's a great alternative to the burger.

2 pounds fresh Salmon fillet
4 ounces Teriyaki sauce
1 small Ginger piece
Black Pepper and Salt

Preheat BGE to 600 degrees.

Mix all in the grinder or food processor.

This mixture will be wet, but the oil in the salmon will hold it together.

Grill approximately 5 minutes a side.

Seafood

Notes:

SALMON TARTARE

3/4 pound fresh Salmon, cut into 3/4 inch squares
2 tablespoons Dijon mustard
1/4 cup Capers, drained
3 tablespoons olive Oil
3 tablespoons Cilantro, finely chopped

Combine all ingredients in a large mixing bowl.

Place in refrigerator for at least 1 hour (2 is better).

Remove from refrigerator and place into cold Martini glasses and serve.

Seafood

Notes:

SALTIMBOCCA

4 Chicken breasts
1/2 pound Prosciutto
1 medium Onion, sliced
1/2 cup parmesan Cheese
Salt and Pepper

Preheat BGE or oven to 375 degrees.

Pound out the chicken breasts to ¼ inch.
To each breast add the Prosciutto ham and cheese along with the onion.
Season and fold the chicken and secure with toothpicks.
Brown in a skillet and finish in the oven.
Serve with your favorite pasta.

Meats

Notes:

SAUSAGE CHILI

1 tablespoon olive Oil
2 pounds andouille Sausage
2 cups Onion, chopped
2 cloves Garlic, chopped
1 can or bottle of dark Beer
1 can Tomatoes, crushed
3 tablespoons Tomato paste
1 teaspoon Sugar
6 cups red kidney Beans drained and rinsed
Salt and Pepper to taste
1 cup cheddar Cheese, shredded, for garnish
1 cup green Onion, chopped, for garnish
2 tablespoons Chili Powder

In a large stockpot over medium heat, warm the oil.

Add the sausage and brown, about 5-6 minutes.

Add the onions, garlic, and, chili powder and cook until the onions are soft, about 4-5 minutes.

Deglaze the pan with about 1/2 of the beer and stir about 1 minute.

Add the tomatoes, tomato paste, sugar, and the kidney beans.

Stir well and bring to a boil.

Lower the heat to medium low and cook uncovered for 30 minutes, stirring often to prevent chili from sticking to the bottom of the pot.

Soups, Stews and Chili

Notes:

SAWMILL GRAVY

1 pound your favorite breakfast Sausage
1/4 cup Flour, all-purpose
2 cups Milk
Salt and Pepper to taste

Cook sausage. When done, remove sausage but save a little of the fat.
Add in the flour and whisk for about 5 minutes, until there are no lumps and the flour is cooked.
Add the milk and continue to whisk occasionally until thickened.
Add sausage back in and adjust seasoning.
Ladle over those hot fresh biscuits you just made.

Sauces/ Dressings and Gravies

Notes:

SCALLOPED POTATOES (IRISH LASAGNA)

3 pounds Potatoes, red or yukon
1/3 cup heavy Cream
1/2 pound Boars Head Honey Maple Ham, cubed
3/4 pound gruyere cheese
3/4 pound fontina cheese

Preheat oven to 350 degrees.

In a large stockpot bring 1 gallon of salted water to a rolling boil.

While waiting for the water to boil, slice potatoes thin - about 1/8 inch (you can use a knife or a mandolin if you have one).

When the water boils, blanch the spuds for about 3-4 minutes.

Take them out of the water and in a buttered casserole dish begin to lay the potatoes on the bottom.

Now add cheese (both).

Then sprinkle on some ham.

Repeat process until all the potatoes are gone or you run out of cheese.

Finish the dish with a layer of the mixed cheeses. Add the cream.

Bake for about 35-45 minutes.

Switch the temp to broil and watch as the cheese bubbles and browns.

Remove and let rest about 10-15 minutes.

This will allow the cream to be absorbed and the dish to cool.

Veggies

Notes:

SCALLOPS WITH WASABI CREAM

With the Wasabi add a little and adjust because it can easily over power you.

12 dry packed Scallops
6 ounces heavy whipping Cream
4 tablespoons prepared Wasabi

In a mixing bowl whip the cream to medium peaks.
Fold in the wasabi and set aside.
Get a heavy bottomed pan very hot.
Add a little oil and begin to sear off the scallops.
Season with salt and pepper.
When seared, plate them and top with wasabi cream.

Seafood

Notes:

SEARED DUCK BREAST

3 medium Duck Breasts
Salt and Pepper to taste
1 pint Blackberries
1/2 cup balsamic Vinegar

Put 1-cup water in a medium saucepan. Bring the blackberries, water and balsamic vinegar to a boil.

Cook about 15-20 minutes.

Strain the sauce into another pot and continue to reduce until thick, like syrup.

Place score marks on the fatty skin side of the duck breast to help render the fat.

Heat a medium sized skillet to about medium.

Place the duck, skin side down, and begin to sear, about 3 minutes.

Turn and cook 1 more minute.

Duck should be cooked to medium rare.

Slice on the bias and nape the sauce on top.

Meats

Notes:

SEARED SALMON SALAD

2 six ounce Salmon fillets, skinless, cut into 1/2" strips
2 tablespoons Chef and The Fatman Spicy Love Rub
1 tablespoon olive Oil
1/2 cup Shiraz
1 bag pre-packaged Salad Greens
Bleu Cheese dressing

Season the salmon strips with the Love Rub.

Heat a large skillet over medium high heat for 2 minutes.

Add the oil and salmon.

Sear for one minute per side (or until center is done).

Add the wine and simmer until evaporated.

Divide the salmon strips evenly onto your favorite salad that has been tossed with bleu cheese dressing.

Salads

Notes:

SEARED SCALLOPS

1 1/2 pounds U 10 Scallops (U 10 is the size of the scallop, bigger is better in this case)
Olive Oil
Salt and Pepper
1 each Pepper (red,green,yellow)

Heat a large heavy bottomed skillet to medium high. Add a little olive oil to just coat the bottom.
Season the scallops with salt and pepper.

Place scallops in oil and begin to sear.

While the scallops are searing, slice the peppers very fine (julienne). They are going to be the bed on which the scallops will rest.
When the scallops are brown on the first side (about 3 minutes), carefully turn over and sear the second side (about 1-1/2 minutes more).
Remove and place the scallops on the peppers.

Seafood

Notes:

SESAME CHICKEN ON A STICK

1/3 cup Soy Sauce
2 tablespoons Honey
1 tablespoon sesame Oil
2 tablespoons Onion, chopped
3 Butterball boneless skinless Chicken Breasts, sliced into 1/4" thick strips
bamboo Skewers
3 tablespoons Sesame Seeds

Preheat BGE or oven to 350 degrees.

In a large bowl combine the first 4 ingredients and stir well.

Slice the chicken breast lengthwise into 1/4 inch thick pieces (about five per breast).

Skewer the chicken slices onto the bamboo sticks and place into a Ziploc bag.

Pour the marinade into the bag and place in refrigerator for one hour (or overnight). Remove the chicken skewers from Ziploc bag and discard the remaining marinade.

Sprinkle the sesame seeds over the chicken and grill over a medium fire for 4 minutes per side (or until cooked through).

Serve warm.

Meats

Notes:

SHRIMP AND MUSHROOM STUFFED FILET

1 whole Beef Tenderloin, cleaned of silver skin
1/2 pound shitake Mushrooms
1/2 pound Shrimp (Wild Georgia Shrimp) (Lobster works also)
3 feet wet Butchers Twine
Salt and Pepper

Preheat BGE to 350 degrees.
Begin by sautéing the shrimp and mushrooms in olive oil and a little butter.
Add salt and pepper.
Lay out your whole filet and remove the silver skin.
Take your knife and butterfly the filet.
Season with salt and pepper.
Add the stuffing, roll back over and begin to tie the filet at the head (big end).
Tie it about every 1 1/2 -2 inches.
Season the outside with salt and pepper.
Place the whole stuffed filet on the preheated egg.
Cook until desired doneness.
LET IT REST at least 15 minutes, covering with foil to help maintain heat.

Meats

Notes:

SHRIMP CAKES

1 pound raw Shrimp (Wild Georgia Shrimp if available)
12 smoked Shrimp (Wild Georgia Shrimp if available)
1 Jalapeno, minced
1/2 bunch Cilantro
1/2 cup Breadcrumbs
1 Egg Salt and Pepper

Preheat BGE or oven to 350 degrees.

Mix all ingredients in a food processor.

Remove from the processor bowl and add to a larger mixing bowl.

Take a good handful and pat out to be a nice big thick cake.

Place on a tray then place tray into BGE. Add a few alder wood

chips to give it a subtle flavor.

Cook until firm. Serve with your favorite sauce.

Seafood

Notes:

171

SHRIMP DOGS

Thanks to the folks at the Wild Georgia Shrimp Association

1 pound 16-20 count Shrimp (Wild Georgia Shrimp if available)
16 wooden Skewers, 1 per shrimp, soaked in water
1 Egg, beaten
1 cup whole Milk
1/2 teaspoon Baking Powder
3/4 cup yellow Cornmeal
1/2 cup Flour, all-purpose
2 teaspoons Sugar

Preheat oil in heavy bottomed pot or fryer to 350.

Mix all the ingredients (not the shrimp and skewers) until a well-blended batter is achieved.

Skewer the shrimp and then place the shrimp into the batter.

Pull up and place shrimp dogs into the oil. Cook until golden brown.

Remove and drain on a paper towel.

Serve with your favorite sauce.

Seafood

Notes:

SHRIMP SCAMPI GENOVESE

This recipe was performed with Father Willy, Kevin Jenkins (The Fatman), Fred Genovese, (The Chef), and Mike Stock, Sous Chef, for the benefit of needy families at St. Brendan's Church in Cumming, Georgia on 12/18/2004 for our Christmas Day show. The volunteers and audience loved it. Gone baby!

2 sticks Butter
Extra virgin olive Oil
2 cloves Garlic, minced
2/3 pound peeled Shrimp (Wild Georgia Shrimp if available) tail on
Salt and white Pepper to taste

Melt butter in a 10" to 12" sauté pan. Add a little bit of olive oil to keep the butter from browning.
Do not brown butter before you add the olive oil.
Add garlic and stir it until it is fragrant and slightly cooked (about 2 minutes).
Add shrimp, salt, and white pepper, stirring until shrimp have just cooked and been coated with the butter garlic mixture.

Seafood

Notes:

SMOKED MUSHROOM PASTA

1 pound rotelle Pasta
2 tablespoons olive Oil
1/2 pound Tasso, chopped
1 tablespoon Garlic, chopped
1 pound smoked Mushrooms
2 1/2 cups heavy Cream
2 teaspoons Worcestershire sauce
1/2 cup parmesan Cheese, grated
Pasta of your choice

Cook pasta until al dente.

Meanwhile in a large skillet over medium heat, add Tasso and cook about 2 min.

Add garlic and onions and cook until fragrant about 30 seconds.

Add the smoked mushrooms (chop the bigger ones).

Stir well and cook for about 30 seconds; then add the cream and reduce by half about 10 minutes.

Then add the Worcestershire sauce and cheese and about 2 tablespoons of butter.

Stir well and serve with Pasta.

Veggies

Notes:

SMOKED PORK BUTT

If you want to add a little more crust, rub in olive oil, and then add spices. This is very simple, but makes the butt oh so tasteful.

4 pound Pork Butt
6 cloves Garlic, minced
Chef and the Fatman Love Rub

Preheat smoker or Big Green Egg to 200 degrees (remember low and slow).

Season the pork butt with Chef and the Fatman Love Rub, or your blend of spices.

Make small slits in the pork and insert the cloves of garlic (studding is the term for this).

Place in smoker and smoke for about 12 hours (internal temperature of 185 degrees), until tender and ready to fall apart.

At this point, wrap in foil and towel or blanket let rest for about 2 - 3 hours.

Pull the pork apart and add sauce if desired.

Meats

Notes:

SMOKED SALMON PATE

12 ounces smoked Salmon, sliced
16 ounces cream Cheese, room temperature
Zest and juice of 1 Lemon
Salt and Pepper

Line 4 small ramekins with plastic wrap.

Line the dishes with the salmon, letting the salmon hang over the edge.

In a mixing bowl, mix lemon juice, zest, cream cheese and leftover salmon until soft.

Spoon the mixture into the salmon bowl.

Cover and refrigerate for 45 min.

Invert onto a plate and serve with Melba toast or pita chips.

Seafood

Notes:

SOFT SHELL CRAB

1 Crab per person (have the fish monger clean your crabs)
3 Eggs
2 cups Flour, all-purpose
2 cups Breadcrumbs
Salt and Pepper

Heat a large skillet to medium high with medium olive oil or canola oil.
Dredge the crabs in the flour, then the egg wash, then into the breadcrumbs.
Place into the oil and cook on each side for about 1-1/2 min.
Drain on paper towels and re-season after removing from the oil.
Serve with remoulade or tartar sauce.

Seafood

Notes:

SOMETHING EXTRA RED BEANS

1 teaspoon olive Oil
1 box Zatarain's Red Beans and Rice
1/2 cup Tomato sauce
1/2 teaspoon Oregano, dried
1/2 teaspoon Basil, dried
1 pinch Thyme, dried
Salt and Pepper to taste
5 teaspoons Adobo seasoning, divided

In a saucepan, combine all ingredients except Red Beans and Rice and 2 teaspoons of the adobo.
Simmer on low heat.
Cook Zatarain's according to box instructions.
When ready, mix rice and other ingredients together.
Add in rest of adobo.

Veggies

Notes:

SOUTHERN BISCUITS

2 cups Flour, all-purpose
1 1/2 teaspoon Baking Powder
1 1/2 teaspoon Salt
2 teaspoon cold Butter
1/2 cup solid vegetable Shortening
1 cup Milk

Preheat BGE or oven to 400 degrees.

In a large mixing bowl combine the flour, baking powder, and salt.
Mix well.

Add 1 teaspoon of butter and the shortening into the dry ingredients.
Stir in the milk.

Dust your work surface with flour.

Take the dough and start folding it into itself about 10 times.

Roll out the dough to about 1 inch thickness.

Using a biscuit cutter or glass, dip it into some flour, then cut out the biscuits.

Place biscuits on a baking tray and let sit for 15 minutes to rest.

Bake for about 15 minutes or until golden brown.

While they bake, melt the rest of butter and brush on top of the hot biscuits when they come out.

Appetizers

Notes:

SOUTHERN CORNBREAD DRESSING

This recipe is from Liz Shepard, Social Circle Ga.

2 1/2 cups Cornbread
4 slices loaf Bread
10 soda Crackers
4 cups chicken/turkey Stock
2 Eggs, hard-boiled
4 tablespoons Butter, melted
1 1/4 tablespoons rubbed Sage
1/2 cup Mild La Victoria Salsa Picante
1 cup Onion, chopped
1 cup Celery, chopped
2 Egg, well beaten
1/2 teaspoon Baking Powder
1 tablespoon Sugar
Salt and Pepper to taste

Preheat BGE or oven to 425 degrees.

Chop hard-boiled eggs.

Mix cornbread, loaf bread, and soda crackers into chicken stock.

Add remaining ingredients. Mix well.

Add Salt and Pepper to taste.

(Dressing will be better if mixture is allowed to stand overnight in refrigerator.)

Pour until 1 1/2" thick into greased, 9" X 13" dish.

Bake until brown and firm, but not hard.

This may be frozen before or after baking.

Sauces/ Dressings and Gravies

Notes:

SOUTHERN STYLE MACARONI AND CHEESE

Recipe by Cheri Zittrauer
This takes a few minutes but it is the BEST Mac and Cheese we've ever had. Take the time.

2 pounds elbow Macaroni
3 cloves Garlic, pressed or diced
1 stick Butter
32 ounce Velveeta Cheese, cubed
2 Eggs, lightly beaten
4 cups Milk or Half and Half
2 cups cheddar Cheese, sharp, grated
1 teaspoon ground black Pepper
1 teaspoon Salt
2 teaspoons ground dry Mustard

Preheat BGE or oven to 350 degrees.
Cook macaroni until tender, in an extra large pot, then drain.

Melt butter and cook garlic until translucent.

Put the macaroni back in the big pot, add the butter and garlic.

Start stirring! Add the cheese and stir as it melts in the hot macaroni stirring, add the milk and egg mixture, salt and pepper and dry mustard.
Stir until all ingredients are well mixed and very creamy.

Pour into baking dishes or pan and top with sharp cheddar cheese.

Bake until browned on top and knife stuck in the middle comes out clean.

Depending on the size of the pan - 20 minutes for a small pan, 30-45 minutes for a large pan.

Serving Ideas: We have found that real butter is one of the mainstays, it holds the flavors together. Margarine just doesn't taste as good. We like real cream but it is really rich, sometimes we use half cream and half milk. Sharp cheddar cheese is important for the sharp flavor; mild cheddar doesn't have the same taste. Of course the best way to insure a great dish to use is cast iron, but even the disposable pans still work well.

Pasta

SOUTHERN TOMATO/HUMBLE PIE

1 cup mozzarella Cheese, grated
1 cup cheddar Cheese, white, sharp, grated
1 cup Mayonnaise
1/2 cup green Onions, chopped
3 heirloom Tomatoes
8 Basil leaves, thinly sliced
1 9-inch "deep" Piecrust

Preheat BGE or oven to 400 degrees.
Peel and slice tomatoes, put into a colander and sprinkle with salt. Let drain 10 minutes.
While tomatoes are draining, bake the piecrust for about 10 minutes.

Mix the two cheeses and mayonnaise together in a bowl and set aside.

Once piecrust is done, remove from oven. Let it cool a few minutes.

Start layering the tomatoes, then basil, and green onions, and repeat until piecrust is full.
Take the cheese mixture and spread on top evenly.
Bake the pie until top is browned lightly, about 45 minutes. Let stand for 10 minutes. Slice and serve.

Veggies

Notes:

SPICY GARLIC EGGPLANT

This recipe comes from friend, Chef/Partner Kong of Atlanta's premier Chinese restaurant Little Szechwan

3 Eggplants, skin peeled in sections (to look like stripes)
2 teaspoon Garlic, chopped
1 teaspoon Ginger, chopped
2 teaspoon Chinese Chili Paste
1 tablespoon Soy Sauce
1 teaspoon white Vinegar
2 teaspoon cooking Oil
1/2 teaspoon Sugar
2 tablespoons Chicken Stock
1 teaspoon Cornstarch mixed with water
1 teaspoon sesame Oil
1 tablespoon green Onion, chopped

Heat deep fryer to 375 degrees.
Cut each eggplant into 3 cross-sections then cut each cross section into 6 strips approximately 2 inches long.
Deep fry pieces until skin turns deep purple (approximately 6 - 8 minutes).

To a medium hot wok, add small amount of oil. Swirl around pan to coat, and then dump out excess. The eggplant will provide plenty of oil in of the fryer, even after being drained.
Add eggplant, garlic, ginger, chili paste, soy sauce, vinegar, cooking oil and chicken stock. Cook for approximately 3 minutes.
Then add cornstarch and water, sesame oil and chopped green onions.

Stir-fry 1 minute.

Serve.

Veggies

Notes:

STEAK SALAD

You can find the recipe for the Red Wine Vinaigrette with Honey in our "Dressings" section.... we wouldn't leave you hangin baby!

1 1/2 pound Rib Eye steaks
1 head romaine Lettuce, cleaned
1 small red Onion, sliced thin
1 head Endive, sliced thin
24 grape Tomatoes
1/3 cup red wine Vinaigrette with Honey, (recipe found in this cookbook)

Cook the steak to a medium rare temperature. Let it rest.
Combine all ingredients into a large bowl, except steak and dressing.
After the steak has rested, cut into strips and place in the bowl.
Mix in the vinaigrette dressing and serve.

Salads

Notes:

STIR FRY STRING BEANS

*This recipe comes from good friend, Chef/Owner Kong of Atlanta's premier
Chinese restaurant Little Szechwan (named to the Top 100 Hundred Chinese
Restaurants in the US by a leading Chinese News Paper).*

1 pound green Beans, ends cut off, washed and dried
1 cloves Garlic, minced
1 teaspoon Ginger, minced
1 teaspoon Szechwan Cabbage (in jar or can), minced (optional)
1 tablespoon dry Shrimp chopped up, (or substitute bacon here)
1 tablespoon Soy Sauce
2 teaspoon white Cooking Wine
1 teaspoon sesame Oil
1/2 teaspoon Sugar
3 green Onions, chopped

Set deep fryer at 375.

Deep fry beans until they wrinkle, approximately 1 - 2 minutes (wrinkles
mean the fiber has broken down).

Remove and drain.

Heat a wok to medium heat.

Add all ingredients except sugar and chopped green onions. Stir until
coated and all ingredients blended.

Add onions and sugar. Stir-fry 30 seconds to 1 min.

Serve.

Veggies

Notes:

T

TASSO SHRIMP AND CREAM PASTA

3/4 stick Butter
3/4 pound Tasso, julienned
1 1/2 cups heavy Cream
2 pounds Shrimp(Wild Georgia Shrimp if available), medium sized
1/2 cup green Onion, chopped Pasta of choice

Melt the butter and add the tasso. Begin to sauté.
Cook for about 10 minutes. Remove the tasso and add the cream to deglaze.
Reduce the temperature and begin to reduce the cream.
When cream starts to thicken, add the shrimp and cook 2-3 minutes.
Add the green onion and the cooked tasso.
Place on top of your favorite cooked pasta.

Pasta, Seafood

Notes:

TERIYAKI MARINADED FLANK STEAK

Recipe provided by Executive Chefs Christopher Effa and Clinton Del Marcelle from the Mondo Mocha Café Doubletree Atlanta Northwest-Windy Hill Marietta, GA

1 Beef flank steak or London Broil as it may be called
2 cups good quality sesame Oil
1/2 cup brown Sugar
1/2 cup Soy Sauce
1/2 cup pickled Ginger
1/2 cup dry Mustard

Preheat BGE to 475 degrees.
Combine all ingredients and submerse the flank steak for 36-48 hours in refrigerator.
Finish on grill or BGE to desired doneness.

Meats

Notes:

TEX-MEX TURKEY CHILI

1 cup Onion, chopped
2 cloves Garlic, minced
1 tablespoon vegetable Oil
1 tablespoon Chili Powder
1 teaspoon Cumin seeds
1 teaspoon Sugar
1 can (8 oz) Tomato sauce
1 can (10 oz) Tomatoes and green Chilies, in juice
1 can (15 oz) red kidney Beans, drained
2 cups shredded cooked Turkey breast
3/4 cup Water

Combine onion, garlic, and oil in a medium sauté pan and sweat until the onion is tender, stirring every minute or so.
Add chili powder and next four ingredients. Stir well.
Cook, uncovered, until slightly thickened, stirring mixture as needed so chili will not stick to bottom of pan.
Add rest of ingredients. Stir well.
Cook, stirring on medium high heat until thickened and heated through completely.
Do not let the chili stick to the pan at this point.
Serve with rice or corn bread or on a freshly baked potato.

Soups, Stews and Chili

Notes:

TOMATO GALETTE

1 sheet Puff Pastry
2 large Tomatoes
5 ounces soft Goat Cheese
3 heads roasted Garlic
Extra-virgin olive Oil

Preheat BGE or oven to 350 degrees.

Roast garlic in oven for about 1-1 1/2 hours until soft.

Let cool. Meanwhile roll out your puff pastry.

Slice your tomatoes and season with a little salt and let set for about 10 - 15 minutes (to pull out some moisture).

In a mixing bowl combine the goat cheese and roasted garlic to form a paste. Add extra virgin olive oil to loosen up the mixture.

Take the goat cheese/garlic shmear and spread onto the puff pastry.

Now top with tomatoes.

Place on a baking sheet and bake for about 20 - 25 minutes.

Cut and serve warm.

Veggies

Notes:

TOMATOES ANTI PASTA

1 large Tomato
1/3 cup Prosciutto, diced
1/3 cup mozzarella Cheese, marinated
1/3 cup Mushrooms, marinated

Cut a wedge into the tomato and clean it out.
In a mixing bowl combine the cheese, prosciutto and mushrooms.
Over-fill the tomato and let it fall out on the plate.
Garnish with a sprig of thyme or oregano.
Add dressing if you like...a nice balsamic would work very well.

Salads

Notes:

TUNA AU POIVRE

This recipe taken verbatim out of Pat Conroy's book "The Pat Conroy Cookbook-Recipes of My Life." You may want to use White Peppercorns. This recipe can be done with a scant 1/4 cup of oil or less in the skillet, or done under a broiler. You may have to correct cooking times to have the tuna come out the way you like it. "This fine recipe prepared and adapted by Chef Fred and Pat Conroy at Rich's/Macy's on 10/02/2004 "The Pat Conroy Show".

1/4 cup Kosher Salt
1/2 cup whole black Peppercorns, coarsely cracked
4 Bluefin Tuna steaks
Vegetable Oil

Combine the salt and cracked pepper in a shallow baking dish and press the tuna into the mixture, covering both sides of each steak.
In a large nonstick skillet, pour enough oil to coat bottom of pan (and thereby cook) the tuna.
Heat the oil over moderately high heat until hot but not smoking. Sear the tuna until a crust forms.
Using a long-handled slotted spatula or tongs, turn the tuna only once; 3 minutes total cooking time for rare; 4 minutes for medium rare.

Seafood

Notes:

TWEAKED DIJON MUSTARD CREAM SAUCE FOR ROULADE

This recipe was performed by Master Chef Tony Seta. He became a quick friend and was appreciative of the show. Shortly after meeting us, he had to move. He is sorely missed in Atlanta.

1 large Shallot, finely chopped
1 tablespoon Butter
2 tablespoons red wine Vinegar
2 tablespoons Dijon mustard
2 pinches Herbs de Provence Spice Mix
1 cup heavy Cream
Salt and Pepper to taste

To make the sauce, in a non-reactive (non-metal) saucepan, melt the butter and sauté the remaining chopped shallot until translucent but not browned. Add the vinegar and reduce most of the liquid.

Add the mustard and cream, and salt and pepper to taste.

Simmer until the sauce thickens to coat the back of a spoon.

Nape (drizzle) on Roulades, serve.

Sauces/ Dressings and Gravies

Notes:

TWO SAUSAGE OYSTER STUFFING

Great for Thanksgiving for a Northeastern touch. However, don't just use it for Thanksgiving. Experiment and you will find that it makes a great side dish.

1 pound pork Sausage
1 pound andouille Sausage
2 pounds Oysters
1 medium Onion, chopped
4 stalks Celery, chopped
5 cups Chicken Stock
1 pound Breadcrumbs

Preheat BGE or oven to 375 degrees.

Remove casing from pork sausage and smoosh into large skillet.

Brown pork sausage until almost done.

Cut andouille sausage into bite size (1/4" - 1/2") pieces, add andouille to skillet.

Cook through.

Drain pan slightly, add celery and onion to same pan and cook about 3 minutes, until almost soft.

In a large bowl combine rest of ingredients, except chicken stock, mix well.

Add just enough chicken stock to moisten the stuffing but not too wet. Remember you can add but you can't take out.

Place the mixture in a buttered casserole dish and bake for about 50 - 60 minutes, uncovered.

To test for doneness, shake pan, it should barely jiggle (culinary term).

If the stuffing is set, let it rest for about 15 minutes covered with foil.

Seafood

Notes:

V

VEAL CHOP MARSALA

1 Veal chop per guest
4 ounces Mushrooms, your favorite variety
3 ounces Vidalia Onion, sliced
3 ounces Marsala Wine
2 tablespoons Butter
Pasta of your choice

In a large medium hot skillet, add a little olive oil and begin to sear the chops.

Brown on each side about 3-4 minutes per side.

When the second side is done, remove the chops and keep warm.

Add a little more oil and sauté the onions and mushrooms.

Remember to season each step as you go along.

When the mixture has sat about 5 minutes, add the Marsala (**BE VERY CAREFUL OF FLAME-UP** take off heat before adding Marsala).

Cook about 4-5 minutes, reducing the wine.

Add the chops back and ladle the mixture on the chops to warm through.

Place chops on beds of pasta.

Add a little butter to sauce and pour over chops and your favorite pasta.

Meats

Notes:

W

WARM SLOW POACHED BUTTER WILD GEORGIA SHRIMP

We love using our "homegrown" and harvested Wild Georgia Shrimp. We refer to them as the Crown Jewels of the Georgia Coast, along with our awesome Georgia Blue Crabs.

1 pound Wild Georgia Shrimp, peeled and deveined, tail on
1 pound Butter, unsalted
3 tablespoons Water
1 Bay Leaf
Hot Sauce (you decide the heat level)
Cayenne pepper (again, you decide the heat level)
4 tablespoons Worcestershire sauce
Zest of 1 Lemon
Juice from zested Lemon
6 grinds fresh white Pepper
1 loaf crusty Baguette
1/4 cup flat leaf Parsley, chopped

In a glass bowl, combine shrimp, hot sauce, and parsley.
Cover and chill for at least one hour. In a saucepan set over medium heat, combine remaining ingredients, except the bread and parsley; combine well.
When the butter has melted, lower heat to medium-low.
Before adding the shrimp, check the seasoning; add as needed.
Add the shrimp. Let sit for 2 minutes.
GENTLY stir the shrimp (remember: low and slow; this is poaching not boiling) for 6 to 8 minutes.
Shrimp should be pink and slightly firm.
Cut the bread on an angle, and place in the bottom of a bowl.
Spoon some shrimp and sauce on top of the bread.
Garnish with parsley.
This dish is very rich, so I suggest you serve it as an appetizer.

Appetizers, Seafood

Notes:

198

WATERMELON CAKE

An awesome recipe from the Cordele, Georgia Watermelon Festival. Try it...you'll like it!

1 package white Cake Mix
1 1/3 cups seedless Watermelon, cubed
1 package mixed fruit Gelatin Powder
3 Egg whites
1 tablespoon Oil

Preheat oven to 350 degrees.

Grease and flour a bundt pan.

In a large bowl, combine dry cake mix, cubed watermelon, gelatin powder, egg whites and oil.

Beat until smooth.

Pour into a prepared pan and bake for about 35 minutes or until a toothpick inserted comes out clean.

Cool on a rack and frost with watermelon icing.

Desserts

Notes:

WATERMELON MARGARITAS

This recipe is one of several performed at the Cordele Watermelon Festival. Truly one of the most fun events with TRUE Southern Hospitality at the Daphne Lodge restaurant. What more could you ask for!

4 cups frozen seedless Watermelon, 1" chunks
4 Lime wedges
Kosher Salt on a small plate
3/4 cup triple citrus Tequila or any good-quality Tequila
1/2 cup Triple Sec
1/3 cup fresh Lime juice

Seed (the little white ones) then freeze 1-inch chunks of watermelon in a plastic bag, until solid.
Run a lime wedge around the rim of a large stemmed cocktail glass and dip the moistened rim in the salt.
Set lime aside for garnish.
Transfer three-fourths of the melon chunks, separating them, to a blender.
Add the tequila, Triple Sec and lime juice and blend.
Add the remaining melon and blend until smooth. Pour.
Squeeze a lime wedge into each cocktail, drop the wedge into the glass, and serve immediately.

Beverages

Notes:

WATERMELON SALAD

This is a great change of pace and a unique salad. Cool and refreshing, just what we need during the "dog days" of a Southern summer or the Cordele Watermelon Festival. Chill baby!

6 cups Watermelon, 1 inch cubes
3 small pickling Cucumbers (small)
1 Jalapeno, seeded, minced
3 tablespoons red wine Vinegar

Mix all together GENTLY and place in refrigerator for 2 hours. Serve.

Salads

Notes:

WHITE TURKEY CHILI

We performed this chili recipe at Bloomingdale's in Atlanta. It was a standing room only show and this was a favorite.

1 tablespoon Oil
1/4 cup Onion, chopped
1 cup Celery, chopped
4 cups cooked Turkey, chopped
2 cans (15.5 oz) great northern Beans, drained
2 cans (11 oz) Corn, undrained can
1 can (4 oz) green Chilies, chopped
4 cups turkey or chicken Stock
1 teaspoon ground Cumin

Heat oil in a skillet over medium heat.

Add onion and celery; cook and stir 2-3 minutes.

Place all ingredients in a large saucepan (at least 4 quarts).

Stir well.

Cover and cook about 15 minutes over medium heat stirring occasionally until thoroughly heated.

Sprinkle mozzarella cheese on top if desired.

Poultry, Soups, Stews and Chili

Notes:

ALPHABETICAL
INDEX

A
APPLE DUFF 2
APPLE SCRAMBLE 3
AWESOME HOT FUDGE TOPPING 4

B
BACON WRAPPED PORK TENDERLOIN 6
BAKED RIGATONI 7
BANANA NUT BREAD 8
BANDITO WINGS 9
BARBEQUE SAUCE FOR SHRIMP SKEWERS 10
BARBEQUED SHRIMP SKEWERS 11
BASIC CHICKEN STOCK 12
BBQ NACHOS 13
BISON MEATLOAF 14
BLACK BEAN SAUCE TOFU 15
BLACKENED FLANK STEAK DEGLAZED WITH WINE 16
BLEU CHEESE TARTAR SAUCE 17
BLOODY MARY LONDON BROIL 18
BLUE CHEESE SLAW 19
BRAISED SEA SCALLOPS IN MARSALA SAUCE 20
BREAD PUDDING 21
BROWNIE SHORTCAKE 22
BUFFALO CRAB STUFFED CHICKEN DRUMETTES 23

C
CAJUN SHRIMP WITH CHEESE GRITS 25
CAJUN STYLE CRAWFISH SCALLION RICE CAKES 26
CALAMARI SALAD 27
CHEDDAR CHEESE SOUP 28
CHEF AND THE FAT MAN "I GOT YOU BABE" NACHO 29
CHEF AND THE FAT MAN "LOVE THAT BLEU CHEESE 30
CHEF AND THE FAT MAN "MANLY" PORK AND BEANS 31
CHEF AND THE FAT MAN AMERICAN ONION DIP 32
CHEF AND THE FAT MAN AMERICAN RED DRESSING 33
CHEF AND THE FAT MAN AWESOME GARLIC BREAD 34
CHEF AND THE FAT MAN BARBECUED SHRIMP 35

K

KAREN'S "FLYING D" CHILI FROM TEDS MONTANA GRILL 105

KD'S BITTERSWEET CHOCOLATE MOUSSE 106

KD'S STEAMED ASPARAGUS WITH LEMON, OLIVE OIL 107

KEY WEST BBQ SAUCE 108

KIELBASA CHOWDER 109

L

LAMB CHOPS 111

LAYERED BLACK BEAN DIP 112

LEG OF LAMB 113

LINDA'S POTATO SALAD 114

LOBSTER BISQUE 115

LOBSTER PASTA 116

LODGE CAST IRON BEEF STROGANOFF 117

LODGE PINEAPPLE UPSIDE DOWN CAKE 118

M

MAPLE BBQ CHICKEN WINGS 120

MARLBORO PIE 121

MARVIN WOODS' FRENCH ONION SOUP 122

MEXICAN CHOCOLATE FONDUE 123

MEXICAN CORNBREAD 124

N

NO BAKE CHERRY CHEESE CAKE 126

NOT YO' MAMA'S BANANA PUDDING 127

O

OLD FASHIONED TEA CAKES 129

ONION BREAD 130

ORANGE TAFFY 131

OYSTER STEW 132

P

PAELLA 134

PAN SEARED VEAL CHOP & MUSHROOM CHIPOTLE CREAM SAUCE 135

PANKO DUSTED FRIED OYSTERS 136

PASTA CARBONARA 137

CATEGORY

INDEX

Appetizers

BANDITO WINGS 9

BBQ NACHOS 13

BRAISED SEA SCALLOPS IN MARSALA SAUCE 20

BUFFALO CRAB STUFFED CHICKEN DRUMETTES
WITH BLEU CHEESE TARTAR SAUCE 23

CAJUN SHRIMP WITH CHEESE GRITS 25

CAJUN STYLE CRAWFISH SCALLION RICE CAKES 26

CHEF AND THE FAT MAN "I GOT YOU BABE" NACHO
CHEESE SAUCE 29

CHEF AND THE FAT MAN AMERICAN ONION DIP 32

CHEF AND THE FAT MAN AWESOME GARLIC BREAD 34

CHORIZO ENCRUSTED SEA SCALLOPS 62

CRAB AND CORN DIP 58

GOAT CHEESE STUFFED SOURDOUGH BREAD 82

GORILLA BREAD 83

HOT CHEESY BEEF DIP 96

HOT CRAB DIP 97

LAYERED BLACK BEAN DIP 112

MEXICAN CORNBREAD 124

ONION BREAD 130

SOUTHERN BISCUITS 179

WARM SLOW BUTTER POACHED WILD GEORGIA SHRIMP 198

Beverages

WATERMELON MARGARITAS 200

Desserts

APPLE DUFF 2

APPLE SCRAMBLE 3

AWESOME HOT FUDGE TOPPING 4

BANANA NUT BREAD 8

BREAD PUDDING 21

BROWNIE SHORTCAKE 22

CHEF AND THE FAT MAN CHERRY CHEESE CAKE
(COOKED) 37

CHEF AND THE FAT MAN COCONUT MACAROONS 38

CHEF FRED'S 5 PUCKER POWER KEY LIME PIE 48

CHEF MIKE'S APPLE CRISP 50

CHOCOLATE BREAD PUDDING 54

CHOCOLATE CHIP PECAN PIE 55
CHOCOLATE CHIP SCONES 56
CRAZY CAKE 63
FLAN 74
FLOURLESS CHOCOLATE CAKE 75
FOUR BERRY COBBLER 76
FUDGE TOPPED BROWNIES 79
GRAHAM CRACKER CRUST FROM SCRATCH 84
KD'S BITTERSWEET CHOCOLATE MOUSSE 106
LODGE PINEAPPLE UPSIDE DOWN CAKE 118
MARLBORO PIE 121
MEXICAN CHOCOLATE FONDUE 123
NO BAKE CHERRY CHEESE CAKE 126
NOT YO' MAMA'S BANANA PUDDING 127
OLD FASHIONED TEA CAKES 129
ORANGE TAFFY 131
PEANUT BUTTER ICE CREAM TOPPING 139
POACHED PEARS 141
RASPBERRY CREME BRULEE 154
ROASTED PEACH BRULE WITH WHITE PEPPER CREAM
SAUCE AND CRUZAN RUM SYRUP 156
WATERMELON CAKE 199

Meats
BACON WRAPPED PORK TENDERLOIN 6
BISON MEATLOAF 14
BLACKENED FLANK STEAK DEGLAZED WITH WINE AND BLEU
CHEESE 16
BLOODY MARY LONDON BROIL 18
BUFFALO CRAB STUFFED CHICKEN DRUMETTES
WITH BLEU CHEESE TARTAR SAUCE 23
CHEF AND THE FAT MAN "MANLY" PORK AND BEANS 31
CHEF AND THE FAT MAN SAUSAGE STUFFED BREAD 45
DRY RUBBED RIBS 66
DUBLIN STYLE CORNED BEEF 67
GRANDMA STOCK'S TENDERLOIN WITH WHITE PEPPER
GRAVY 85
HORSERADISH AND BLEU CHEESE ENCRUSTED RIB EYE 94
ITALIAN SAUSAGE BURGERS 101
ITALIAN SAUSAGE STUFFED BELL PEPPERS 102
ITALIAN SAUSAGE WITH PASTA 103

KAREN'S "FLYING D" CHILI FROM TEDS MONTANA GRILL 105
LAMB CHOPS 111
LEG OF LAMB 113
LODGE CAST IRON BEEF STROGANOFF 117
MAPLE BBQ CHICKEN WINGS 120
PAN SEARED VEAL CHOP & MUSHROOM CHIPOTLE CREAM
SAUCE 135
PASTITSIO 138
PICADILLO 140
PORK LOIN WITH SPINACH AND ANDOUILLE SAUSAGE 143
PORK ROULADE (SERVED WITH MUSTARD SAUCE) 144
PORK TENDERLOIN WITH POMEGRANATE SAUCE AND
BACON 145
POTATO CHIP CHICKEN 147
POTATO PORK SKILLET 149
SALTIMBOCCA 161
SEARED DUCK BREAST 166
SESAME CHICKEN ON A STICK 169
SHRIMP AND MUSHROOM STUFFED FILET 170
SMOKED PORK BUTT 175
TERIYAKI MARINADED FLANK STEAK 188
VEAL CHOP MARSALA 196

Pasta
BAKED RIGATONI 7
FRESH PASTA 77
LOBSTER PASTA 116
PASTA CARBONARA 137
PASTITSIO 138
SOUTHERN STYLE MACARONI AND CHEESE 181
TASSO SHRIMP AND CREAM PASTA 187
Poultry
BANDITO WINGS 9

BASIC CHICKEN STOCK 12
CHEF FRED'S DANCING HERB ROASTED CHICKEN 49
GREEK ISLES MARINADED CHICKEN 86
GRILLED CHICKEN WITH SMOKED MUSHROOMS 87
PAELLA 134

WHITE TURKEY CHILI 202

Salads

BLUE CHEESE SLAW 19

CALAMARI SALAD 27

CHEF AND THE FAT MAN "LOVE THAT BLEU CHEESE SALAD DRESSING" 30

CHEF AND THE FAT MAN AMERICAN RED DRESSING 33

CHEF AND THE FATMAN RANCH STYLE DRESSING 47

CHICKEN AND SHRIMP JAMBALAYA SALAD 52

CHIPOTLE SLAW 53

HORIATIKI SALATA (GREEK PEASANT SALAD) 93

LINDA'S POTATO SALAD 114

SEARED SALMON SALAD 167

STEAK SALAD 184

TOMATOES ANTI PASTA 191

WATERMELON SALAD 201

Sauces/ Dressings and Gravies

BLEU CHEESE TARTAR SAUCE 17

CHEF AND THE FAT MAN AMERICAN RED DRESSING 33

CHEF AND THE FAT MAN GREAT GIBLET GRAVY 41

CHEF AND THE FAT MAN MUSTARD BBQ SAUCE 43

CHEF AND THE FAT MAN RED BBQ SAUCE 44

CHEF AND THE FAT MAN TOMATILLO SALSA 46

CRANBERRY ORANGE COMPOTE 60

GREEK ISLES MARINADED CHICKEN 86

HARVEST TOMATO VINAIGRETTE 91

HOMEMADE BBQ SAUCE 92

HOT PEPPER SAUCE 98

KEY WEST BBQ SAUCE 108

QUICK MARINARA 152

RED EYE GRAVY 155

SAWMILL GRAVY 163

SOUTHERN CORNBREAD DRESSING 180

TWEAKED DIJON MUSTARD CREAM SAUCE FOR ROULADE 193

Seafood

BARBEQUE SAUCE FOR SHRIMP SKEWERS 10
BARBEQUED SHRIMP SKEWERS 11
BRAISED SEA SCALLOPS IN MARSALA SAUCE 20
CAJUN SHRIMP WITH CHEESE GRITS 25
CAJUN STYLE CRAWFISH SCALLION RICE CAKES 26
CALAMARI SALAD 27
CHEF AND THE FAT MAN BARBECUED SHRIMP 35
CHEF AND THE FAT MAN CRAB STUFFED MUSHROOMS 39
CHICKEN AND SHRIMP JAMBALAYA SALAD 52
CITRUS SHRIMP 57
CRAB STUFFED PRAWNS 59
CRAWFISH AND RICE DRESSING 61
FISH TACOS 71
FISH TEQUILA TACOS 72
FIVE SPICE CRUSTED SALMON 73
GRILLED SHRIMP TOAST 89
LOBSTER PASTA 116
OYSTER STEW 132
PAELLA 134
PANKO DUSTED FRIED OYSTERS 136
POACHED SNAPPER WITH COCONUT SAUCE 142
POTATO ENCRUSTED SEA BASS 148
POTATO WRAPPED SALMON 150
SALMON BURGERS 159
SALMON TARTARE 160
SCALLOPS WITH WASABI CREAM 165
SEARED SCALLOPS 168
SHRIMP CAKES 171
SHRIMP DOGS 172
SHRIMP SCAMPI GENOVESE 173
SMOKED SALMON PATE 176
SOFT SHELL CRAB 177
TASSO SHRIMP AND CREAM PASTA 187
TUNA AU POIVRE 192
TWO SAUSAGE OYSTER STUFFING 194
WARM SLOW BUTTER POACHED WILD GEORGIA
SHRIMP 152
WILD GEORGIA SHRIMP PO BOY 81

Soups, Stews and Chili

BASIC CHICKEN STOCK 12
CHEDDAR CHEESE SOUP 28
CHEF AND THE FAT MAN "MANLY" PORK AND BEANS 31
CHEF AND THE FAT MAN BRUNSWICK STEW 36
CHEF AND THE FAT MAN EASY BUT DELICIOUS CHILI 40
CUCUMBER SOUP 64
ESCAROLE SOUP 69
KAREN'S "FLYING D" CHILI FROM TED'S MONTANA GRILL 105
KIELBASA CHOWDER 109
LOBSTER BISQUE 115
MARVIN WOODS' FRENCH ONION SOUP 122
ROASTED PUMPKIN SOUP 157
SAUSAGE CHILI 162
TEX-MEX TURKEY CHILI 189
WHITE TURKEY CHILI 202

Veggies

BLACK BEAN SAUCE TOFU 15
CHEF AND THE FAT MAN HEAVY GREEN BEAN
CASSEROLE 42
CHEF MIKE'S CHINESE GREEN BEANS 51
FRIED GREEN TOMATOES 78
GRILLED EGGPLANT POCKET 88
HORSERADISH MASHED POTATOES WITH CARAMELIZED
ONIONS 95
ITALIAN POLENTA 100
KD'S STEAMED ASPARAGUS WITH LEMON, OLIVE OIL
& PARMESAN 107
POTATO AND MUSHROOM GRATIN 146
SCALLOPED POTATOES (IRISH LASAGNA) 164
SMOKED MUSHROOM PASTA 174
SOMETHING EXTRA RED BEANS 178
SOUTHERN TOMATO/ HUMBLE PIE 182
SPICY GARLIC EGGPLANT 183
STIR FRY STRING BEANS 185
TOMATO GALETTE   190